Principles of

Macroeconomic Literacy

Principles of
Macroeconomic Literacy

John Scott
University of North Georgia

UNG
UNIVERSITY of
NORTH GEORGIA™
UNIVERSITY PRESS
Dahlonega, GA

Published by:
University of North Georgia Press
Dahlonega, Georgia

Printing Support by:
Lightning Source, Inc
LaVergne, Tennessee

Cover design by Corey Parson

ISBN: 978-1-940771-18-2

Printed in the United States of America, 2015
For more information, please visit ung.edu/university-press
Or email ungpress@ung.edu

Contents

SUMMARY OF THE ENTIRE TEXT

People try to make themselves better off by interacting with each other in the economy. By engaging in production and trade, individuals create value for themselves and for society at large. Problems often arise, which people solve as best they can. People are best able to solve their own problems because they know their abilities and their preferences for goods and services better than others know them. If people are forced by others, who do not know them as well, to take actions that are against their own judgment, production and trade will become less efficient, so value is destroyed and they will end up with fewer goods and services—food, medical care, shelter, clothing, transportation, information, and entertainment—than they would have had if they had been free to choose for themselves. They will live shorter, more miserable lives.

As you read, you will find links to stories, documents, and sound and video files on the web. Some of them are for reference only and will be marked as [reference]. Others are [essential]. **Essential links may contain test material.** References to Bastiat's work are always essential. The following story introduces some concepts that are necessary to understand the logic of the course.

Story: The Best Thing

After Ramona asked Greg to have a seat across the desk, he said, "I'm not working hard enough to suit you because I'm not going to work at your pizza place for the rest of my life."

She pursed her lips to keep from smiling. "So what better thing are you going to do with the rest of your life?"

Trays banged in the kitchen. Jen was mad that they left her with cleanup.

"I'm waiting," Ramona said.

"Well," he said. "Nobody asked me before, but I've thought about it a lot. Here's what I want to do—the most valuable thing I can possibly do."

Ramona tapped a nail on her desk. "How do you know *this* isn't the most valuable thing you can do?"

"Because I can get another job—maybe better. And after I graduate, I'll be able to do even better."

"Is it just money? Is that all value is to you?"

"No," Greg said. "It's not just money."

She threw up her hands. "Then what?"

He sat back in the chair. "Let me ask you a question. Why don't you double my pay?"

She laughed. "Because there are lots of guys out there that will do your job for what I pay you—maybe some would do it better and maybe some would do it for less money. And, besides, if I doubled your pay, I'd have to charge more for pizza, then Papa John's would end up selling all the pizza in town, and you wouldn't have your high-paid job for very long. You know they'd be glad to put me out of business."

Jen yelled from the kitchen, "I could use some help in here."

He crossed his ankle over his knee and knitted his fingers behind his head. "So you're saying that how much I make is based on how much people are willing to pay for pizza—and, heck, Papa John's doesn't pay any better than you. Sounds like your value for me is all about how much pizza I can make and how much you sell it for—just money."

She pointed as she said, "Of course I *love* your sparkling personality."

"So pay me more."

She rolled her eyes. "I don't love it *that* much."

He looked up at the ceiling. "So I guess it *is* about money. If I find somebody willing to pay me more, it's because I'm doing something that people really want—really value."

"You could volunteer to help people at the hospital, couldn't you? Wouldn't that be more valuable?" Ramona asked.

He smirked. "Hospitals have plenty of money. If they're not willing to pay someone to help out, they must not care about the work that person is doing."

"I'll make you a deal. If you don't make yourself more valuable to me, you can go find somebody that values you more. And if you make yourself way more valuable to me for the next six weeks, you get a raise. Deal?"

Jen stood in the doorway, hands on hips. "Any time now."

Greg sighed and trudged after her.

Economic Decisions

Economics is all about decision making. Economists have studied how to make decisions about how many kids to have, how criminals should be punished, and whether to vote. They also study decisions you usually think about—like whether to buy a fuel efficient car, which profession someone should choose, and how much of a product a company should produce.

Economics is the discipline that studies how efficient decisions are made. Any efficient decisions, in any field, are analyzed through the economic way of thinking. **Efficient decisions** involve choosing the most valuable alternative.

VALUE/BENEFIT

Thinking Exercise 1.1: Value Concepts

What is the value of each of the following?

Five quarts of motor oil

Five quarts of blood

Five Snickers bars

Your answers should be numbers that are useful for all decision making—and not just among the three alternatives above. In formulating your answers, consider the contrast between the following.

- What is the value of each?
- What is price of each?
- What is the cost of each?
- What is the most you would pay for each?

You might write down the answers for each in the table.

Table 1.1

Item	Value	Price	Cost	Most You'd Pay For
5 Qts Motor Oil				
5 Qts Blood				
5 Snickers Bars				

- You should probably start with the easy ones and work to the harder ones.
- As you do so, you might ask, "What does this concept mean?" Come up with a meaning and answer each one consistently with that meaning.
- You may also wonder about situations. The situation is the one in which you find yourself at this minute.
- Remember, your answer to "Value" must be one that is useful in making all decisions.

If given the opportunity to choose one of the three options in Thinking Exercise 1, which would it be? If you would choose the blood, you'd have to figure out what you'd do with it, where you'd keep it, etc.

Most people in the here and now would choose the Snickers bars. Even if they don't like them they could give them to a friend. And if you would choose the Snickers bars, then the value that you wrote down for the Snickers Bars must be the highest of the three. Our choices reveal our values—this is called the **theory of revealed preference**.

If you did the exercise, you may have discovered some things like the following **characteristics of value**.

- Value depends on the situation.
- Value is different for different people.

Thinking Exercise 1.2: A Third Characteristic of Value

Here is what I mean by the third characteristic. At a party, there is all the pizza that everybody there can possibly eat. It's good stuff, and they keep making more, fresh.
- What is the value of the first slice to you?
- What is the value of the second slice to you?
- What is the value of the twentieth slice to you?

How does the value change as you eat more slices?

Does this work for
- Value of the first umbrella, second umbrella, third umbrella you own?
- Miles driven this week?
- Value of the first car, second car, third car you own?

The point of Thinking Exercise 2 is to help you see the third **characteristic of value**. Here it is, along with the other two.

- Value depends on the situation.
- Value is different for different people.
- Subsequent units of the same good have less value.

One reason that this is usually a characteristic of value is that we naturally put each unit to its best use. So if you have an umbrella, you might put it behind your front door. A second umbrella might go under the seat in your car. If the best place to place an umbrella were under the seat, you'd have put the first one there. What about a third umbrella? A fourth? The idea that we first choose the best, then the second best, and so on, is called the **optimal arrangement principle**.

The same logic holds for miles driven. If you could only drive 20 miles, you'd drive the most important 20. If you could drive another 20 miles, you'd put the next batch of miles to the next-best use, so its value would be less. Eventually, you would not have much reason to drive any farther.

A second reason, which is not as compelling as the optimal arrangement principle in many cases, is that many appetites get satisfied as we consume more. When you have eaten a lot of pizza, eating any more is actually painful.

Measuring Value

Now, let's go to a different exercise—one that helps put a dollar number on value.

Thinking Exercise 1.3: Numerical Value

Which would you rather have:

- A Snickers bar
- 40 cents

If you'd rather have the Snickers bar, what does that say about its value?
If you'd rather have the 40 cents, what does that say about the Snickers bar's value?

After answering those questions,

- Formulate a procedure to determine the exact dollar value of a Snickers bar for yourself.
- Formulate a procedure for determining the value of a single Snickers bar to a class of students.

The point of Thinking Exercise 3 is to give you a method to measure value. The **value of something to an individual** is the most that individual is willing to sacrifice to obtain that something. Or, if the individual owns that something, its value is the least the individual is willing to accept in exchange for that something.

Sometimes this is hard, but that does not mean it's impossible.

- Economists find the value of clean air by looking at how very similar houses' prices vary in neighborhoods with clean air and in polluted air.
- Economists get guidance as to the value of a potential child to its parents by looking at how much must be sacrificed in time and money to have and raise a child (the cost—around half a million dollars).
- Economists even find how much individuals probabilistically value their own lives by looking at how much money a worker will accept to work at a job where they are more likely to get killed. This value is between $1 million and $10 million—a large variation, but is not unlimited. http://www.theglobalist.com/the-cost-of-a-human-life-statistically-speaking/ [reference]

Nearly everyone will claim that there are things that are beyond price. However, most economists say that—other than what someone would pay save their own life or the life of someone close to them, with certainty—nothing is beyond price. For instance, if the life of a child is beyond price then we should make sure school busses have shielding from meteorites. Even though deadly meteor strikes are rare, the priceless value of a child's life would mean that no expense is too much.

We can measure value in dollar terms, but we do not really value "dollars." Dollars are pieces of cotton with dye/ink on them or are bits and bytes in our bank accounts. The only reason we value dollars is because of the stuff we exchange them for. So it is fine to keep track of prices, profits, and losses in terms of dollars. But what is really going on is that we are making choices about time and energy, about goods and services. With good economic theory, we can always remove dollars from the analysis and still be left with sound reasoning.

Reading Exercise 1: Reread the story just before the chapter—The Best Thing. Notice how the different values are related. Write a multiple choice question based on a value concept.

Read the introduction, Chapter 1 (paragraphs 1.1-1.21), and Chapter 4 (1.58-1.81) of Bastiat's essay, *What is Seen and What is Not Seen* at http://www.econlib.org/library/Bastiat/basEss1.html [Essential]

- Does Bastiat think that theater and the fine arts have value?
- What does Bastiat say about how "productive" the theater is? What does he mean by "productive?"
- Does Bastiat conclude that if the fine arts have value that government should support the fine arts? Why or why not?
- What does Bastiat say about abolishing the fine arts?
- What does Bastiat say about the jobs that government support for the fine arts creates?
- What does Bastiat mean by "The workers will be fortunate if there are a few crumbs left for them!"

COST

Economics is all about efficient decision making. Efficient decision making involves choosing the most valuable alternative. But when one chooses the most valuable alternative, they give up something. The **cost** is the value of *the best* alternative which is sacrificed when a decision is made.

The last sentence includes the words "the best." Here is an example that points out why "the best" is there.

What is the cost of coming to class today? Suppose these are the alternatives and their values.

- Come to class
- Work $9
- Sleep $8
- Play Call of Duty $6

For this person, the cost of coming to class today is $9, which is associated with work—it is the most valuable alternative sacrificed in order to come to class. Cost is *not* the sum of the values of all of the things you could possibly do, because you cannot do all of them.

Should this person come to class? We don't know. It depends on the value of coming to class. And remember the characteristics of value—they all apply here. We could further complicate the example by saying that the person works across the street from home, but must drive for 20 minutes to get to class. This would mean that the cost of coming to class would be higher because of sacrificed driving time and gas money.

Costs may or may not involve spending money. If you skip work, you do not have to pay the employer—it's just that the employer does not pay you. Playing *Call of Duty* has value to people, else they would not do it. But they don't have to send more money to Activision to pay for playing during the hours in which they are skipping class.

Thinking Exercise 1.4: Cost Mental Exercise

For you, now, what are the costs of:
- A bread pretzel?
- A second bread pretzel?
- At an all-you-can-eat deal like Cici's Pizza, eating another slice of pizza?
- Finding a new job?
- Getting a university diploma?
- Having a child?

Reread "The Best Thing." What costs do the characters discuss?

Since any decision has at least two alternatives, choosing an alternative means that one must sacrifice at least one other alternative. That is, any decision involves costs. This is called the **no free lunch** principle. Think about it in those basic terms—how could anyone possibly have a free lunch? First of all, when we say "free" we mean no cost *for anybody*. No one has to give up anything. So if your friend buys you lunch, that's not free. There is still a cost. It's just that someone else is paying it. Suppose you go hunt in the woods for berries and plants. You are using time and energy, so that lunch is not free either.

Politicians like to talk about the value of alternatives, without talking about the cost. They constantly act as if there is a free lunch. Much of the time they either ignore the cost or shift the cost to others. It is much easier to shift the cost than it is to reduce the cost.

Macroeconomics—the study of entire economies, using concepts like total output, the unemployment rate, the national debt, total investment—is so large that sometimes it is easier to try to hide the fact that there are costs. But resources must be used if we want to produce a good (like a road) or a service (like police protection) and those resources could have been used in other ways. We have many more wants than our resources can satisfy—this is called **scarcity**. So someone pays the cost. Public roads, parks, and education are not free, even if there is no user fee. If we do not pay for resources such as the construction worker, the land, and the teacher, they will go do something else.

DECISIONS

If we assume that these are the only factors involved in coming to class today, we can talk about which decision this person will make.

- Come to class $12
- Work $9
- Sleep $8
- Play Call of Duty $6

This person will come to class. The cost of coming to class will be $9. This person will gain $3 in value by coming to class, rather than choosing the next best alternative—work. (Note: to simplify, we're assuming there's no problem with travel time, etc. This person apparently works and sleeps really near to class.)

Thinking Exercise 1.5: Decision Making Examples

Consider the following decisions using the decision making framework:
- At an all-you-can-eat deal like Cici's Pizza, eating another slice of pizza
- Finding a new job
- Getting a university diploma
- Having a child
- Volunteering at a hospital

Marginal Decisions

Much of the time we do not choose all or nothing.

- To eat pizza or not
- To buy gasoline or not
- To study or not

We choose how much of something to do.

- How much pizza to eat
- How much gasoline to buy
- How much time to devote to study

For these decisions, called "marginal," or "at the margin," we need the third characteristic of value, developed in Thinking Exercise 2. Subsequent units of the same good have less value. The **Marginal Value** of something is the value of the individual units of that something. To speak with precision, we usually speak of the marginal value of a particular unit—like the 21st gallon of gas you use this month.

Entries in the following table are individual slices of pizza—the 1st, 2nd, 3rd, etc. **Not** 1 slice, 2 slices, 3 slices, etc. The values are measured as in Thinking Exercise 3—what a person is willing to pay for the individual slice. Since these are values for individual slices, we call them marginal values. By the third characteristic of value, these marginal values fall as more pizza is consumed.

Table 1.2

Slice	Marginal Value
1st	$4.00
2nd	$3.50
3rd	$3.00
4th	$2.50
5th	$1.50
6th	$.50
7th	-$1.50

How much pizza should this consumer eat?

Some people respond, "It depends on how hungry the person is."

But they're wrong in that. The values in the table tell us precisely how hungry the person is, if we understand what marginal value is. So how much should the consumer eat?

This is a trick question. This individual is willing to pay $4 for the 1st slice of pizza. But how much *must* they pay? That is, what is the *cost* of a slice of pizza? That has not been given yet.

We are going to act as if we can measure the cost in dollars—so the consumer is able to hand over dollars and get slices of pizza. This example would be more complicated if we were worried about how much time it took to eat, but for simplicity's sake, ignore that for the moment. The cost of the pizza to the consumer in this example is the price.

Suppose the price is $2.75 per slice. Should the consumer eat the first slice? The second slice? The third slice? This person is willing to pay $4.00 for the first slice so if the price is $2.75, then they're willing to buy the first slice. Since this person is willing to pay $3.50 for the second slice, if the price is still $2.75, then they're willing to buy the second slice. We consume each unit for which the marginal value is at least as great as marginal cost—that is, we are use **marginal analysis**. Using this method, we can see that the consumer should buy the third slice, too. The most they're willing to pay for the fourth slice is $2.50, but they'd have to pay $2.75. So they would not buy the fourth slice. So the answer to the question is, "if the price were $2.75 per slice, this consumer would buy three slices."

Some people object that the consumer should stop after the first slice, since it is the most valuable. But as long as the consumer is willing to pay more than what they have to pay, they're willing to buy more.

What if the pizza were free? Many people respond that "they should eat until they get full." But using the values above, we can figure out what that number is. Free pizza means the price is $0.00. And that means this person will eat six slices. Ponder this question: "Is there any way to get this consumer to eat the seventh slice?" We can graph the relationship.

Figure 1.1

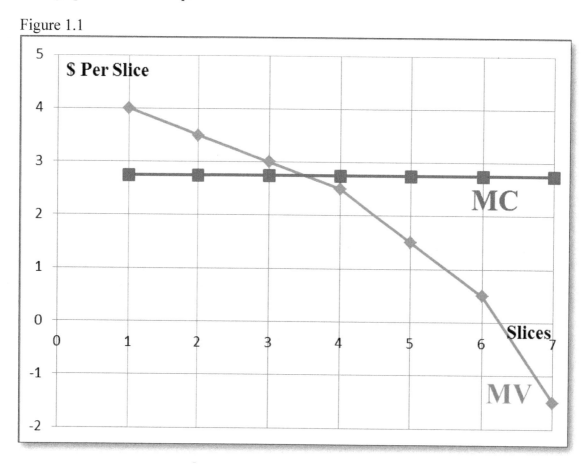

From this, we can see that the blue values of pizza are greater than the red costs of pizza for three units, but not for the fourth. If the price of pizza fell, the red line would move downward and the two lines would intersect at a higher number of slices. If the red line moves upward, the opposite happens. If this consumer could buy partial slices, they would buy part of the fourth slice. And at CiCi's pizza, where you pay a flat fee to eat all the slices you want, the red line would be on the horizontal axis. So this consumer would eat six slices and part of a seventh.

The True Shape of Marginal Costs I–The Consumer

We previously assumed that costs to the consumer were the same as price. But we can do better than that by realizing that every time a consumer puts another dollar toward pizza consumption, the consumer takes that dollar from consumption of something else. The consumer will take that dollar from its least valuable use—like a dollar spent on a Redbox DVD—not from a highly valuable use, like rent. Then, if the consumer spends a second dollar on pizza, the consumer takes that dollar from the *second* least valuable use for the dollar. As the consumer spends more on pizza, the value that is sacrificed (which is, by definition, the cost) rises. You may have noticed that this is another example of the optimal arrangement principle.

Figure 1.2

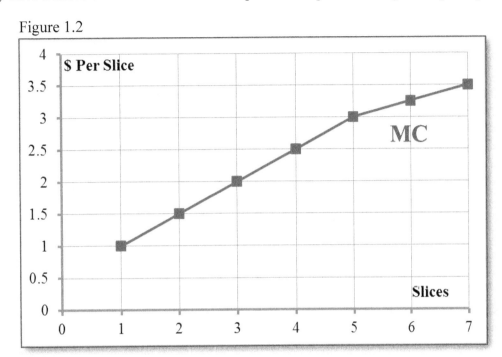

Thinking Exercise 1.6: Study Time

- What are the benefits of an hour of study? Of a <u>second</u> hour of study? Of a <u>third</u> hour?
- As hours of study rise, what happens to the value of the marginal study hour?
- Explain what is meant by the cost of study.
- As hours of study rise, what happens to the cost of the marginal study hour?
- Draw a graph and address this statement: "A student can never study enough."

The True Shape of Marginal Costs II–The Producer

Story: The Worst Thing

Ramona said, "You two have griped long enough about not having enough help here, so I did some hiring. I expect lots more pizzas to be sold."

Gregg looked up from the pan he was spreading dough in. "Thank you! Will they be working tonight? After the ball game, we'll be swamped."

"Yeah, they'll be here. All twelve of them."

Jen said, "Twelve more? We're going to have fourteen people working in this place tonight?"

Ramona put her hands on the sales counter and leaned toward them. "Yup. So I expect that since you'll have seven times as many workers, you'll make seven times as much pizza."

"You're kidding." Gregg said.

Jen threw her hands up. "Where will we put them all? There's not room for that many workers in this place. We'll be lucky if we make twice as many pizzas as usual."

Ramona said, "You're very creative. You'll figure something out." She pulled her inventory clipboard out from under the sales counter and went into the back.

Jen put her face in her hands, smelling bell pepper on them and wondering if her eyes were going to start stinging. "Those are going to be the most expensive pizzas we ever made. I should just quit now."

As we add workers to a production facility, eventually they become less productive because there's no way for everyone to take part in the production process. This is called the **Law of Diminishing Returns**. If the facility could expand instantly, this might not happen, but facilities cannot expand instantly. As we put the fifth, sixth, seventh worker to work in the pizza place, and they become less productive, the small amount of pizzas they add to the process cost a lot.

Suppose a worker can add 12 pizzas per hour to the process and suppose workers are paid $12/hour. This means that the labor cost of the pizzas is about $1 each. But a subsequent worker can only produce 4 more pizzas per hour, so the labor cost of those pizzas is about $3 each. *So as production increases, marginal cost rises.* The previous MC graph suffices as an illustration of this.

Thinking Exercise 1.7: Jobs

Are jobs costs or benefits to society?

What does Bastiat say about different kinds of jobs in Chapter 4?

http://www.econlib.org/library/Bastiat/basEss1.html [essential]

SUPPLY AND DEMAND

Understanding Demand and Supply Separately

Demand is the relationship between the possible prices of something and the quantities people are willing to buy, all things being equal.

If you turn back to the previous discussion of marginal value, you have a discussion, a table, and a graph that fulfills the definition of demand. For any price, you can find the quantities that this person wants to purchase. If you want to find the total quantities that many consumers in a market want to purchase at each price, you only need to add up those individual demand curves. So *the demand curve is the same as the marginal value curve.*

Demand can change—if either more or fewer people are in the market or if the individuals already in the market have higher or lower values. So if the surgeon general announces that pizza prevents cancer, some people would probably value it more highly, moving the demand curve upward vertically—that is, to the right.

Supply is the relationship between the possible prices of something and the quantities that people or firms are willing and able to sell, other things equal.

Many might say that the minimum that a seller will insist on, in order to supply a unit, is something above cost. They say this because they think of cost only in terms of money spent. But our definition and explanation of cost indicates that cost includes more than money spent. It includes all that is sacrificed in order to do something.

Thinking Exercise 1.8: Cost, Revisited

A rich friend of your parents bought an item on Craig's List from someone in Atlanta and they would like to have it in hand by the end of the day. So they offered to pay your full cost of picking it up. You know they have plenty of money and don't mind paying for your service in driving to Atlanta, finding the place, and transporting the item to them. So you can discard the idea that you should do a favor for them. It is strictly business.

List all the components of the cost of picking up and delivering the item—the list should include everything that you should reasonably be compensated for.

Since cost includes time, trouble, and all other sacrifices, the minimum amount someone will accept to do something is the cost of doing that something. Yes, more is always preferred to less, but when push comes to shove, the cost is the bottom line.

This means that the marginal cost concept is the same as the supply concept. Parts of the supply decisions of producers are internal—they'd rather be doing something else, so they face the optimal arrangement principle with costs, as previously explained. However, the law of diminishing returns is also relevant to decisions like making and selling pizza, where the tradeoffs are external—between individuals.

Supply can change if firms' costs change because either the prices of their resources change or the technology *that is economically efficient to use* changes. Some advanced technologies are not economically efficient to use—so suppliers who used them would have high costs and could not survive competition with lower cost competitors.

Putting Supply and Demand Together

It is crucial to realize that this section uses value and cost in specific ways. Previously, we looked at an individual making a decision. If the individual was a consumer, the benefits involved getting satisfaction from consuming and the cost involved items like the price of the product. *But the price of the product is a benefit to the producer, not a cost,* and to the producer the cost involved items like time and money sacrificed to produce but the benefit involved items like the price of the product.

This section discusses *markets*. Supply and demand curves have already been derived. When this section says "suppose cost rises," it refers to the cost to the producer—it does not refer to the price of the product.

Observe in the graph below that if the price of the good is $3.50, producers will be willing to supply 7 units, but consumers will only want to buy 2 units, creating a surplus of 5 units.

Figure 1.3

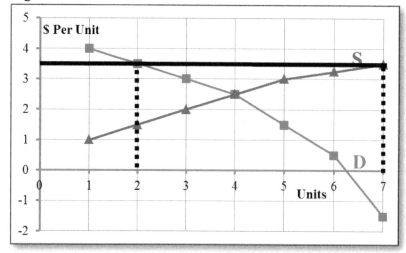

This makes sense because at high prices suppliers are very willing to supply, but consumers are not very willing to buy. For the opposite reasons, a price of $1.50 creates a shortage of 3 units, as seen below.

Figure 1.4

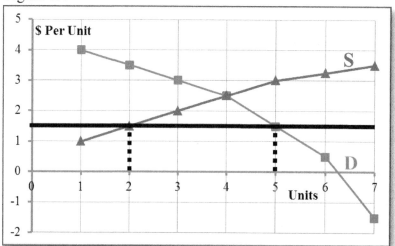

If the price were $3.50, causing the surplus, producers would eventually have to lower their prices to get rid of the surplus. If the price were $1.50, the shortage would cause consumers to form long lines, waiting for the product to be available. They might tell sellers that they are willing to pay more if they can just depend on buying the good. In any case, sellers see that they can charge more and still sell all they are producing. Only at a price of $2.50 do neither of these things happen. At the **equilibrium price** of $2.50, consumers can buy all they want and, at the same time, firms can sell all they want.

Figure 1.5

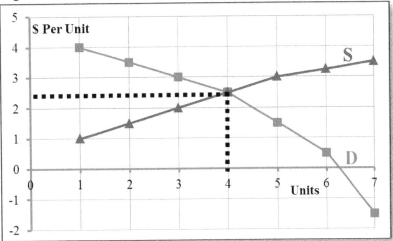

OVERALL WELLBEING

Thinking Exercise 1.9: Total Value, Total Cost, Social Gain

Table 1.3

Slice	Marginal Value	Marginal Cost	Total Value	Total Cost	Social Gain
1st	$4.00	$1.00	$4.00		
2nd	$3.50	$1.50	$7.50		
3rd	$3.00	$2.00			
4th	$2.50	$2.50			
5th	$1.50	$3.00			
6th	$0.50	$3.25			
7th	-$1.50	$3.50			

This table shows the marginal values to the consumer and the marginal costs to the producer.

- Fill in the last three columns.
- I started the process already. If the value of the 1st slice is $4.00 and the value of the 2nd slice is $3.50, then the <u>Total Value</u> of the first two slices is $7.50. Continue similarly for the rest of the column.
- Do the same for the Total Cost column, remembering that each marginal cost is the cost of an individual unit—the 1st, the 2nd, the 3rd, etc.
- **Social Gain** = Total Value - Total Cost
- Fill in the Social Gain column.
- Where is the greatest social gain?
- Compare this answer to the previous graph, under Putting Supply and Demand Together.
- Try and explain why this works.
- You probably noted some ambiguity with your answer. Try and resolve the ambiguity by supposing that we can make and sell fractional units—half a unit, 1/4 of a unit.

First we will look at individual units, then we will consider the whole market working smoothly, not in blocky units. Someone is willing to pay $4.00 for the first unit. Someone is willing to make and sell the first unit for $1.00. So the first unit will be made and sold. The social gain from this unit will be SG = MV - MC = $4.00 - $1.00 = $3.00. (Note that the social gain from an individual unit is called the marginal social gain). We don't yet know how much of this social gain goes to the consumer and how much to the producer if we don't know the price that will be charged, but we know that they will be able to agree on a price since the value is greater than the cost.

Someone is willing to pay $3.50 for the second unit. Someone is willing to make and sell the second unit for $1.50. So the second unit will be made and sold and the marginal social gain from that unit will be $2.00. This increases the overall social gain.

As long as the value of a unit is greater than the cost, the overall social gain increases as more is produced. This happens until the fourth unit is produced. If we leave the market free, the value and cost of the last unit will be $2.50 and the total social gain is maximized. At the equilibrium price, each unit produced has a value at least as great as the cost. The graph below uses the numbers in the table to illustrate how much of the gains go to the producer and the consumer at the equilibrium price.

Figure 1.6

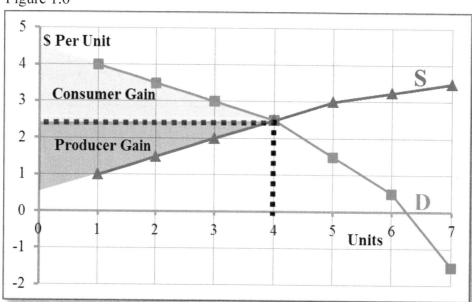

Thinking Exercise 1.10: Apportioning Gain to Consumer and Producer

- Look back at Thinking Exercise 1.9.
- Given that the price will be $2.50 and that 4 units will be sold, how much in total is paid by consumer to producer?
- Find the **Consumer's Gain** = Total Value - Total Amount Paid
- Find the **Producer's Gain** = Total Amount Paid - Total Cost

If we eliminated markets and had a central decision maker, we would want to use our resources to produce the things we most value. If we like cars more than trains, we want steel to produce many more cars than trains and track. If corn is efficient for food, but not efficient for fuel, then we want corn to be eaten, not used for fuel.

But free markets do these things automatically. Because the people who must pay are the same people who receive the rewards, the decisions that are made balance out these payments and rewards in the best way that individuals can find. In this way, free people, interacting in markets solve **the economic problem**— allocating scarce resources to their best uses.

MARKET ADJUSTMENTS

Supply and demand can shift, based on changes in market conditions.

> **Changes in supply** are shifts in the supply curve. That is, producers wish to produce more or less, *even if the price does not change*. They are caused by changes in the producer's costs.

> **Changes in demand** are shifts in the demand curve. That is, consumers wish to buy more or less, *even if the price does not change*. They are caused by changes in things that influence the consumer's willingness to purchase the product which have nothing to do the product price.

Beginning students often use these concepts incorrectly. They say, "supply is how much is available," and "demand is how much people want." In doing this, they omit the crucial concept that producers will make more available at higher prices and consumers will want more at lower prices. That is, once supply and demand have been constructed, as above, beginning students wish to ignore that construction and rely, instead, on simplifications that often mislead.

> **Thinking Exercise 1.11: Changes in Demand and Supply**
>
> How do the following things increase or decrease demand? Supply? Or do they do neither?
> - In the market for steak, the price of cattle feed rises.
> - Increased use of robotics lowers the cost of producing automobiles.
> - In the market for pizza, student incomes increase.
> - In the market for chicken, the price of beef falls.
> - The state hands $50 to anyone who buys an internet connection.
> - The state creates a new agency requiring oil workers to document each action they take.

Two Examples

(1) **A new technology has lowered the cost of producing oil.** Using hydraulic fracturing, called "fracking," firms drill to extract oil and natural gas from land where it was previously unprofitable to drill. The graph below depicts the market before fracking. Carefully consider how fracking will change the market with regard to supply, demand, price, and quantity of oil.

Figure 1.7

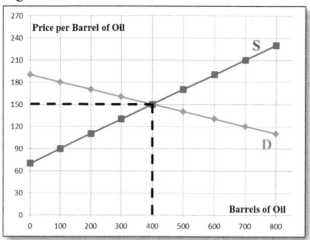

Fracking lowers production cost, which raises supply—moving it to the right. We can look at this process in two ways, but both give us the same picture. Lowering the cost of producing a unit shifts the supply curve downward in a vertical direction. But, this means that firms are willing to supply more at the old prices— which means that supply has moved to the right. It is the same movement—and we call it an increase in supply, shown below.

Figure 1.8

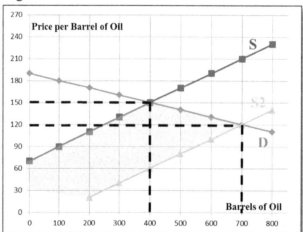

With lower costs, of producing, we are better off, giving rise to the increase in social gain, shown in green. Some of these gains to go the producer and some of them go to consumers, due to lower prices and higher quantities available. Resist the temptation to say, "With more oil available, people will demand more, so demand increases." This is an incorrect statement. Also resist the temptation to say, "There will be a shortage," or, "There will be a surplus." As long as prices are free to adjust, shortages and surpluses, defined above, are eliminated.

(2) What would happen if the government gave each student $2,000 to go to a university?

The graph below depicts the market for a university education with no government financial aid.

Figure 1.9

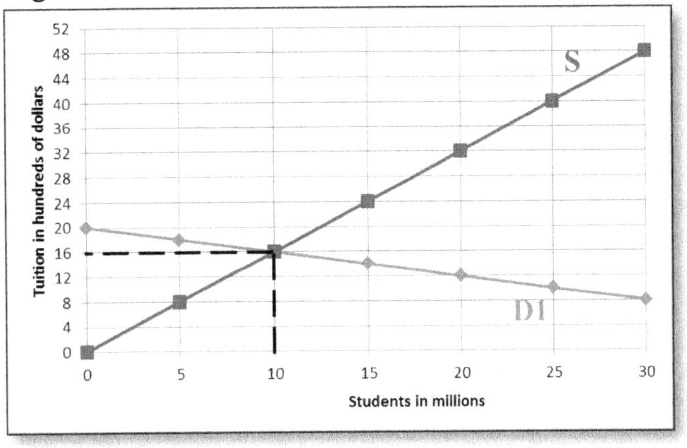

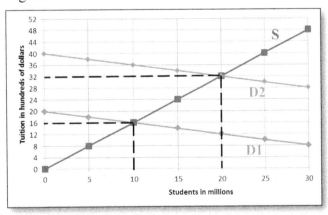

At the old equilibrium tuition of $1,600 there were 10 million students enrolled, reflecting their willingness to pay for education. Since the $2,000 can only be used if enrolled in the university, each student's willingness to pay rises by $2,000. This means that now if universities raised tuition to $3,600, the same 10 million students would be willing to enroll, as shown below—demand rises, vertically by $2,000, to D2 (this does not mean universities *will* charge $3,600).

With the $2,000 aid payment, more students would desire to enroll at the $1,600 tuition. If universities keep tuitions the same, they will have a huge shortage of space (On D2, how many students would want to enroll at a tuition of $1,600?) Universities would have an incentive to raise tuition. On the following graph, tuition rises to $3,200 and 20 million enroll. With the extra tuition money, universities expand their payrolls and the number of buildings, along with administrator positions.

Figure 1.10

For many, this is seen as an excellent outcome. However, those students who were not going to the university before were likely less interested in getting a degree. So the extra 10 million students are not as high quality as the previous 10 million. Professors may adjust by failing more students or by inflating grades, which, in the long run, will lower the value of the degree.

Many students will say, "Without aid I could not afford to attend the university." They are correct as far as they can see. Bastiat cautions us with regard to only taking account of what we can see. What these students do not see is that because of government aid, tuition is higher. So without government aid the university would not be as expensive as students expect.

Also, what students do not see is that someone is paying for this aid. Students who work have higher taxes in order to pay for the aid, as do their parents, who may also be helping support them while they get an education. If we examine the true cost and benefits to the education, we see that for the extra 10 million students, the costs of serving them (on the supply curve) outweigh the benefits (on the *original* demand curve), creating a loss to society. The government is encouraging people to go to the university by paying more than the degree is worth to those students.

Figure 1.11

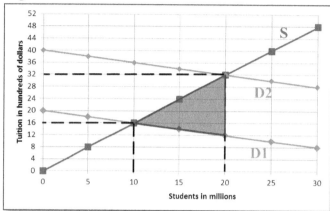

Government Decision Making: Public Choice

INCENTIVES

The previous chapter discussed individual decision making and market results. Markets encourage producers to use resources wisely because that is the most profitable way to produce. If firms are inefficient in their production methods or in their resource choices, they make lower profits and cannot survive in competitive markets. Markets encourage consumers to spend wisely, so that they get the most enjoyment from their incomes.

So if we leave prices free to adjust and leave consumers and producers free to transact, they end up maximizing the gains to society from production. If a third person were to pay and a fourth to receive the reward, then the efficiencies of the market would be destroyed. No outside bureaucrat or dictator can improve on this situation. One of the great economists of the last century, Milton Friedman, in *Free to Choose*, said there are four ways to spend money.

Table 2.1

Whose Money is Spent?		On Whom is Money Spent?	
		On Yourself	*On Someone Else*
	Yours	Care how much you spend and buy what is most valuable	Care how much you spend but don't know the recipient's highest value
	Someone Else's	Don't care how much you spend but buy what is most valuable	Don't care how much you spend and don't know the recipient's highest value

So when individuals pay the costs and receive the benefits of their actions they act efficiently, getting the best they can with limited incomes. And, since business works in the same way, when their owners are responsible for their own costs and benefits, they use resources efficiently.

Free market prices function to:

- **Ration goods to consumers who most want them.** You could buy more gasoline by giving up other things. If you valued gasoline more than the other things, you *would* give up those things and buy more gasoline. For instance, if you got a well-paying job that was further away, you would value gasoline more. If government decreed that gas stations give gasoline away without charging a price, then commuters might not find gas to drive to school or to work, while people who have do not have anything better to do than camp out at gas stations and joyride afterward, would top off their tanks.
- **Give incentives to producers to satisfy consumers.** If oil prices are high, oil companies will spend more on exploration. If oil prices are low, they will not spend nearly as much. If drug prices are high, pharmaceutical manufacturers will spend more on research.
- **Give incentives to conserve scarce resources.** Helium is now getting relatively scarce, so the price of helium balloons is rising. This gives consumers and producers incentives to conserve. It also gives producers incentives to find substitutes for helium, and to recycle helium, which further conserves the scarce gas.
- **Transmit information throughout the economy, as explained below.**

KNOWLEDGE IN SOCIETY

Free market prices will perform the above functions, combining the knowledge of millions of people. The rulers of the state cannot possess this knowledge because they cannot fit it into their minds. Even if one could enter all this knowledge into a computer, by the time the task was done, conditions of value and scarcity would have changed, so a good part of the data would be wrong.

For instance, part of the state's knowledge would concern individuals' preferences, which only the individuals know—the state does not how know to fund the music that you like, or it may not fund music at all. And even if the state knows which purchases you make, it does not know which ones you would have made if prices had been different.

To manage the economy, the state would also need to know how to do every job in the economy. How many US senators know how to herd sheep, build a search engine like Google, manufacture iPhones, or style hair? And even if the state knows how iPhones are made, it does not know how they would have been made if the scarcity of materials changed—which happens all the time. If the state is to improve on the market, then politicians must know this information better than people who do these jobs. This is known as "**the calculation problem.**" Freidrich Hayek, one of the top three economists of the last century, put it this way.

[T]he problem of a rational economic order is determined precisely by the fact that the knowledge of the circumstances of which we must make use never exists in concentrated or integrated form but solely as the dispersed bits of incomplete and frequently contradictory knowledge which all the separate individuals possess. The economic problem of society is thus not merely a problem of how to allocate "given" resources—if "given" is taken to mean given to a single mind which deliberately solves the problem set by these "data." It is rather a problem of how to secure the best use of resources known to any of the members of society, for ends whose relative importance only these individuals know. Or, to put it briefly, it is a problem of the utilization of knowledge which is not given to anyone in its totality.   *Hayek*

http://www.econlib.org/library/Essays/hykKnw1.html [reference]

The state may have an energy plan, a financial plan (a financial plan for their subjects—their own finances are often in deficit), an education plan, and other plans. On this subject, Hayek said,

[W]ho is to do the planning? It is about this question that all the dispute about "economic planning" centers. This is not a dispute about whether planning is to be done or not. It is a dispute as to whether planning is to be done centrally, by one authority for the whole economic system, or is to be divided among many individuals . . . . Which of these systems is likely to be more efficient depends mainly on . . . which of them we can expect that fuller use will be made of the existing knowledge.   *Hayek*

Hayek's appeal to **spontaneous order**, that people organize themselves and interact efficiently, if given freedom to do so, was, perhaps, first enunciated by Zhuangzi, who lived in the third century BC.—"good order results arise spontaneously when things are let alone." http://mises.org/daily/1967 [reference]

Individuals who interact in markets have advantages over state planning:

- Freedom is agreeable to most people.
- Markets utilize the ingenuity of millions of minds.
- There are millions of small market experiments, each with low risk.
- In markets, there is competition to serve others.
- In markets, there are incentives to use resources efficiently.

The major advantage of the state is the use of force. Even the founding fathers of the United States, who were not fond of being governed with a heavy hand, realized that some force was necessary. For instance, markets do not produce national defense because it cannot be individually consumed. So the state threatens force unless citizens pay to maintain the military. The citizens, in general, want defense, so they may consent to some use of force to pay for it. Frederic Bastiat said, "For a nation, security is the greatest of blessings. If, to acquire it, a hundred thousand men must be mobilized . . . it is an enjoyment bought at the price of a sacrifice."

If we wished to test whether markets or state control work better in controlling economic activity, we could draw an arbitrary border across a country, let one part be free and let the other part be controlled by the state. This might be seen as insane, cruel, or simply fanciful. Fortunately for us, the experiment has been done for us— hence it is called a **natural experiment**. Unfortunately for those experimented upon, things do not turn out well.

Figure 2.1

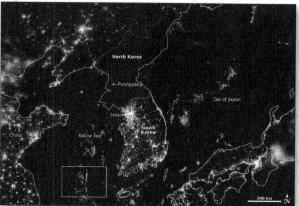

http://earthobservatory.nasa.gov/NaturalHazards/view.php?id=79796 [reference]

This is the area around North Korea and South Korea, with the borders superimposed over a satellite view, by night, from space. South Korea is mostly free, while North Korea is one of the world's most controlled societies. The leadership of North Korea would prefer that their people have housing, warmth, and food, if, for no other reason, they would be better workers and soldiers. But they cannot both control the economy and have abundance.

East Germany and West Germany had the same type of border drawn, with similar results. Some complain that this compares a more free economy with a less free and badly managed economy—that for a good comparison, one should compare a free economy to a less free, well managed economy. But for Hayek's reasons, quoted above, less free states tend to be badly managed.

Here is the general picture for the world. The horizontal axis is a measure of economic freedom of a country, devised by the Wall Street Journal and the Heritage Foundation. The vertical axis is the average income of people in the country. You can see that the general trend is positive—more free countries are materially well off. This material well-being is not really about dollars. It's all about food, clothing, medical care, housing, transportation, communication, and all the other things that economies produce. And understanding free markets starts with the idea of value, and people making choices, interacting, to find more value in life.

Figure 2.2

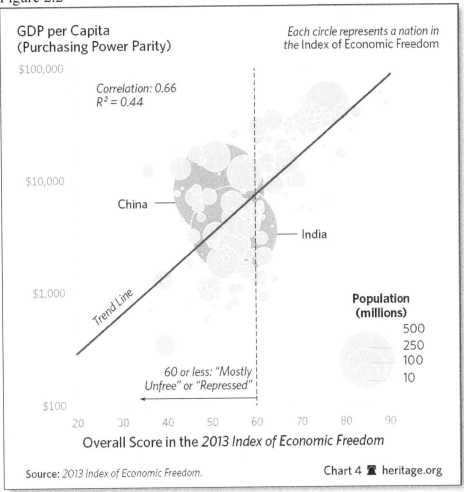

http://thf_media.s3.amazonaws.com/index/pdf/2013/Index2013_Highlights.pdf [reference]

PUBLIC CHOICE

Read Bastiat's Chapter 3 (Taxes) at http://www.econlib.org/library/Bastiat/basEss1.html [essential]

The first chapter of this text contained the theory of how individuals make efficient decisions about consuming, producing, and trading and how they interact with each other. In this chapter we look at how the state makes choices.

This text previously assumed that private individuals are trying to accomplish their goal of getting the most from what they have—their time, talents, and other resources. We make the same assumption about individuals who make decisions for the state, such as politicians and bureaucrats—they are self-interested, caring about their job security and paychecks just as much as anyone else does. As Frederic Bastiat said,

"If the natural tendencies of mankind are so bad that it is not safe to permit people to be free, how is it that the tendencies of these organizers are always good? Do not the legislators and their appointed agents also belong to the human race? Or do they believe that they themselves are made of a finer clay than the rest of mankind?"   *Bastiat*

Although Bastiat enunciated key principles of public choice theory, James Buchanan, a Nobel Prize winner, is usually acknowledged as the founder of the modern "**public choice school**" of economics, which explores how self-interested government employees make decisions.

To be elected to public office, one does not have to be the smartest, the wisest, or the most compassionate. Election to high office requires a set of skills involving time management and salesmanship, including the ability not to say the wrong thing, to avoid responsibility, to tell people what they already believe, and to avoid taking stands that may prove to be unpopular. Few people have these skills in abundance and only those who are the very best at these skills are elected to high office. But these skills are unrelated to being smart enough to tell others how to manage their material affairs. In fact, many economists who study individual decision making all their lives say that they are not able to manage the material well-being of others. As Hayek said, "The curious task of economics is to demonstrate to men how little they really know about what they imagine they can design." http://www.libertarianismo.org/livros/fahtfc.pdf [reference]

Hayek further said that we should not expect that politicians will likely leave individuals alone. "Why the Worst Get on Top," is a chapter in Hayek's book, *The Road to Serfdom*. In it, he says, "the democratic statesman who sets out to plan economic life will soon be confronted with the alternative of either assuming dictatorial powers or abandoning his plans." So if politicians think that tobacco, raw milk, or credit cards are bad, they are likely to make them illegal and not trust individuals to manage their own lives. Their only alternative to using force to carry out a plan to change individuals' behaviors—to arrest people for selling raw milk or loose cigarettes, for instance—is to give up the plan.

RATIONAL IGNORANCE

If voting made any difference, they wouldn't let us do it. — Mark Twain

One reason that the worst can rise to the top, even when people vote on their elected representatives, is explained by the theory of rational ignorance. You probably do not know the best way to find water in the Gobi dessert. And you are probably not interested in looking it up. We are all ignorant of countless bits of information. Perhaps you are ignorant of the comparison between the Hyundai Elantra Coupe and the Honda Civic Coupe—with regard to looks, safety, reliability, gas mileage, and the like. But if you were in the market for a car similar to those, you would likely find out. You might search the web for ratings, look for horror stories about either of them, and the like. But for now, it is probably rational for you to be ignorant of this comparison.

In 2012, the vote totals in Georgia were

- Romney   2,070,221
- Obama   1,761,761
- Johnson   45,056

And votes in the closest election for the US Congress from Georgia, the 12th district, totaled

- Barrow   138,965
- Anderson   119,857

Consider self-interested potential voters in these elections. To vote, they must take time to register and to vote. But in order to make a good choice, they would need to look at the record of the incumbents, listen to the platforms of the incumbents, and try to figure out how much truth they are hearing from each. Some of the issues are complicated and these voters might require more education in order to understand those issues.

If one of those voters had said, "I don't have time for all that," and stayed home, that voter's material well-being would have changed two simple ways. First of all, given the huge numbers of votes separating the candidates, the election results would <u>not</u> have changed—the same candidate would have won. Second, the person <u>would</u> have saved time and trouble by not paying attention and not analyzing the issues, and by staying home. So <u>not</u> voting will almost certainly improve this voter's well-being.

The probability that an individual vote will decide an election, even in congressional elections, is smaller than winning the lottery. And lottery tickets only cost $1, whereas the time commitment of being an educated voter is many times higher, even for people who make minimum wage. And even if a person cast the winning vote in a congressional election, it might make no difference in any legislation over the following two years, since that legislator also casts one of many votes on legislation.

Therefore, many people choose **rational ignorance**—refusing to expend resources to gather information that will almost certainly <u>not</u> lead to a change in the quality of life. Further, since even those who take the trouble to vote are unlikely to change anything, many vote without knowing anything about the candidates—even whether those candidates have, in the past, supported things those voters like. In general, old people vote more, because they have a low cost of their time, while young people with higher costs of their time, vote less.

In markets, consumers seek out information that is valuable. They might try a product, not like it, and never buy it again. But they would pay the price of their mistake. So markets encourage consumers to be informed about things that affect them. But, while a consumer has the power to refuse to buy a bad product, the individual voter, as previously explained, has almost no chance of throwing out a bad politician or changing a bad policy. Since it is not in the voter's interest to find out whether they are voting well, market outcomes are almost always more efficient than voting outcomes. Voters can make the same mistakes over and over, at nearly zero cost.

The rational ignorance model is meant to explain behavior in terms of self-interest. This text does not advocate either voting or abstention. Some decide it is futile to vote in elections in which ignorance dominates the outcome. Others feel a patriotic duty to vote, even so.

Many people are ignorant of rational ignorance and feel that it is likely that they will "win the voting lottery." Many think that since voters, as a group, determine the election, that the individual voter determines the election. In this, they fall prey to the **fallacy of division**—thinking that what is true for a group must be true for all the individuals of the group.

Some rational ignorance theorists have likened voting to cheering for one's favorite sports team. It is a fun activity for some people—not for all—and will not make any difference in the team's performance. Economists have even found that people who display team logos on their homes or cars are more likely to vote.

METHODS OF CHOOSING ALTERNATIVES

Free markets allow **individual choice**, where individuals decide for themselves.

Authoritarian Choice involves a single individual or governing body making decisions for the populace. The decision maker(s) may be elected or not. If the decision maker is elected, rational ignorance insulates the decision maker from paying the price of making policy that harms the public.

Democratic Choice is an authoritarian choice made by individuals voting on decisions for the entire populace.

Authoritarian choices are not the same as free market outcomes because everyone is bound by others' decisions which are enforced by violence or the threat of violence by the state. For instance, with free markets, individuals might decide whether or not to eat salty foods, smoke marijuana, or sell lemonade on street corners. With any other type of choice, the above activities may be prohibited—and have been prohibited in the US, by the voting majorities or by elected representatives. Mark Twain described it this way,

> When you set aside mere names and come down to realities, you find that we are ruled by a King just as other absolute monarchies are. His name is The Majority. He is mighty in bulk and strength . . . . He rules by the right of possessing less money and less brains . . . . than the other competitor for the throne, The Minority. Ours is an Absolute Monarchy.
>
> *Twain*

INTEREST GROUPS

Frederic Bastiat said,

> A man does something that produces good effects equal to ten [dollars], to his profit, and bad effects equal to fifteen [dollars], divided among thirty of his fellows in such a way that each of them [pays] only one half [dollar]. In the total there is a loss, and there must necessarily be a reaction. We must concede, however, that it will be all the longer in coming because the bad effects are spread out so widely among the masses, while the good are concentrated at one point.
>
> *Bastiat*

Here are three examples of special interest groups and how much they cost consumers.

- Since there are so few sugar farmers, the $2 billion that consumers pay in higher prices due to US laws restricting sugar imports and restricting domestic production, only costs each person $2 billion/312 million = $6.41/year. For a family of four, that's a little over $25/year. That's not enough for any individual to campaign against.
- Restrictions on ethanol raise the price of corn by 30 percent. One study revealed that ethanol increased food and fuel prices by about $100/household per year.
- The Cheverolet Volt costs taxpayers $80,000 per car—in addition to the purchase price of $40,000 for the purchaser.

The list of special interest favors goes on, so the total is huge. The presence of interest groups means that individuals are forced to spend their resources on goods they do not want. Each single item is usually small, but, in total, they make the typical household much poorer, in order to make these industries and companies who contribute to campaigns richer. Safe interest groups concentrate gains on a few individuals, so they are small and more easily tolerated and overlooked. A counterexample so the "small/successful" principle is the largest interest group—old people. Social Security and Medicare are 1/3 of the federal budget. It survives because

- Old people, who draw benefits, vote.
- People nearly old enough to draw benefits also vote.
- Many view the program a retirement program, contrary to its structure and legal status.

A special interest might make a $10,000 campaign contribution to a candidate, who then rewards the donor by helping to pass a law to give the donor $10 million in subsidies. In a free market, no one would hand a person $10 million if they were only getting $10,000 in return. But, since the candidate is not spending her own money, it is rational for the candidate to take part in the transaction. These campaign contributions are only illegal if it can be proven that the two parties stated that the contribution was only given in return for the subsidy. Usually the contribution takes place, then the special interest's proposal for the subsidy arrives later.

A rationally ignorant public usually only notices special interests when there are arrests and trials—when illegality is alleged—not when they pay for ethanol in their gasoline. Generally, legislators propose to solve special interest problems by increasing supervision of themselves. That is, the accused write the laws to catch the accused, even though the biggest special interest problems usually involve legal conduct.

Another solution to interest groups burdening the economy is limiting state power. If the state has no ability to hand out favors, no interest group is willing to give campaign contributions to gain the state decision makers' favors. This solution is only possible if voters loudly call for decreased state power. But (1) some people like big government and (2) the rationally ignorant are not interested in learning how much they are harmed.

REGULATION

The <u>original meaning of regulate</u>, as used in the US Constitution is "to make regular." That is, that trade must not restricted by individual states. <u>Today, regulation means "control."</u> We may desire some of the benefits of regulation, but we must always consider the cost.

As discussed previously, firms try to be efficient with resources because it is more profitable for them to do so. Therefore, if the state changes the way firms use resources, costs must rise because firms cannot legally use resources efficiently. At any time in an economy or an industry some firms are doing well, some are barely making it and some are dying. Picture the money that comes into a firm as a building and the cost of the firm as the water level. Some firms are far out of the water—with high profits—some firms are near the waterline, and some are just below the water level. Regulation can raise the level of the water, destroying some firms—that is, destroying value in the economy ("value," as in Chapter 1). Less regulation can lower the level of water, making it possible for new firms to thrive.

Figure 2.3

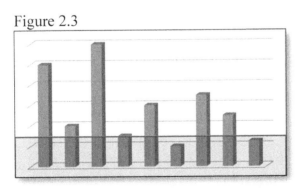

In 2014 Toyota moved from California to Texas, citing a business friendly environment in Texas. This is like moving from a "high water" state to a "low water" state, where it is easier to survive. California Governor Jerry Brown said, "We've got a few problems, we have lots of little burdens and regulations and taxes. But smart people figure out how to make it." These burdens, regulations, and taxes include:

- Texas is a "right-to-work" state. In California employees who work in a unionized company are forced to pay union dues and cannot bargain directly with the company.

- Energy prices are 50% higher in California because of requirements to use some solar and wind generated electricity, which is much higher in price.
- Gasoline prices are 70 cents higher in California.
- California's state income tax is 13.3%. Texas's income tax is 0%.

http://www.sacbee.com/news/business/article2597298.html [reference]

When the "regulatory water" is too high in every state, firms move out of the United States.

Cost of Regulations

The costs of regulation can be broken down into these components.

- **Direct costs of regulation**
  - **Government administrative costs**—sacrificed in order to pay government employees to monitor the regulatory program and enforce the statutes.
  - **Compliance cost**—how much must be sacrificed by the regulated entity to follow the law, which includes reporting costs, planning and administrative costs, and consulting costs.
- **Indirect Costs of Regulation**—results from changes in behavior of firms and individuals due to the regulation, including
  - value of output that is not produced due to the regulation, and
  - wasteful activities that the regulation encourages, such as spending resources to hire lobbyists, to avoid the regulation, or to take advantage of loopholes that are inefficient, except for the regulation—like expensive tax shelters.

CAFE Standards Example

Regulation restricts choices of consumers and producers. For instance, CAFE standards (Corporate Average Fuel Economy) force auto manufacturers to maintain high average fuel efficiency. Without CAFE standards, some consumers would choose more fuel efficient cars and others would choose cars that had characteristics that were more important to them—cheaper, roomier, safer, more powerful, etc. Over the past decades, General Motors has excelled at making larger vehicles—large trucks, vans, etc. But the CAFE standards forced GM to make small cars, which they did not make as well, and therefore had trouble selling. This caused financial problems for General Motors.

The previous chapter established that demand is based on how much consumers value a good and supply is based on how expensive the good is to produce. It also established that free market prices balance off the cost of resources used with the value of the good to the consumer. People are willing to pay for cars that get better gas mileage, so companies will produce those cars voluntarily. CAFE regulations distort the market by forcing companies to produce cars they are not efficient at producing—using resources wastefully. CAFE regulations also reduce the supply of large vehicles that consumers would buy if there were a higher supply, which lowers prices.

In the free market, the car company seen below would produce three million small cars and five million large cars. These amounts are based on consumers' values for those cars and the skills and resources used by the company. It maximizes the company's profit and maximizes the value that consumers get from buying their cars, as discussed in Chapter 1. Part of the value of small cars comes from consumers wanting higher fuel efficiency.

Figure 2.4

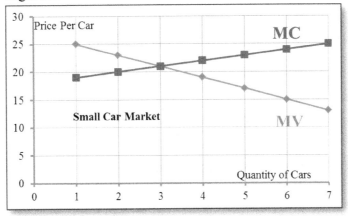

Figure 2.5

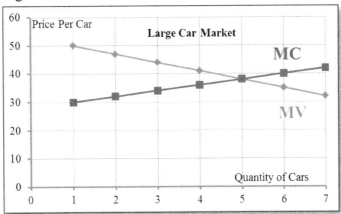

Now government-enforced CAFE standards force this company to increase fuel efficiency, which, for now, can only be done if the company produces twice as many small cars as large cars. Since the firm was maximizing profits and consumers were getting the most value for their money before, they cannot do so now. Suppose this company decides to increase production of small cars from three million to six million. Since the extra cars cost more than people are willing to pay, consumers and producers are worse off. Social gain falls, as seen in the graph, so we are poorer.

Figure 2.6

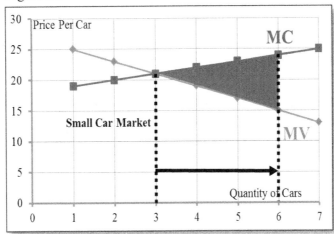

Since the government forces this car company to produce twice as many small cars as large cars, they reduce their large car production from five million to three million, as seen below. Since the company stops producing some cars that people valued more than their cost, consumers and producers are worse off. Social gain falls, as seen in the graph, so we are poorer.

Figure 2.7

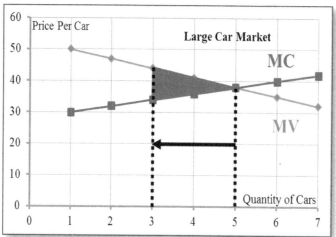

In this example it looks as if the number of jobs might increase or decrease, depending on how many people it takes to make each kind of car. However, your readings of the theater chapter of Frederic Bastiat's essay should tell you that even if auto employment increases, the question of *value* is still the important one. If there is less value, overall, people must be worse off. If CAFE regulations create auto jobs, they, first, destroy value in the auto industry, as shown above. But as auto industry employment increases, workers must move from efficient parts of the economy into the, now, inefficient auto industry. This destroys value elsewhere—in the same way that Bastiat's high value agricultural workers move to jobs producing low valued theater entertainment. Note that Bastiat says that such entertainment is low valued only because people were not voluntarily willing to pay for it.

The free market creates and destroys jobs as well, but in the market this is based on value. We now use steel to produce more automobiles and fewer trains because people value automobile travel more than train travel, so there are fewer jobs making trains and laying track. In order for regulation to improve the economy, the state must overcome the calculation problem in the section above and the incentive problem discussed above.

Finally, as stated, General Motors is victimized by CAFE standards more than most companies since they have not been highly successful at producing and selling small cars. Part of their best solution, given harmful regulations, is to build their small cars in Europe, where consumers are more receptive. So in this case CAFE standards destroy some jobs at home and send other jobs to Europe.

The state introduced CAFE standards during a time when oil was seen as scarce and the public feared higher future prices of gasoline. Since then the state has severely restricted oil drilling, has restricted refinery construction, has passed numerous laws mandating "boutique blends" of gasoline which reduces refinery efficiency, and has mandated the use of ethanol—all of which increase the price of gasoline. The state passes these contradictory regulations constantly, the result of rational ignorance, inefficiency of authoritarian choices of elected officials, and interest group politics.

Ethanol Example

The state requires certain amounts of gasoline sold to be blended with ethanol, which is typically made from corn. The government gives tax breaks and makes direct subsidy payments to corn growers and ethanol manufacturers, equal to approximately half the cost of manufacturing ethanol in order to give them an incentive to produce this gasoline additive that the market does not support due to its inefficiency.

If ethanol were cost-efficient to add to gasoline, refineries would add it without being forced to by government mandate. Since they do not, clearly ethanol increases their costs. Chapter 1 makes clear that the marginal cost curve is the supply curve. In the graph below you can see the result of raising costs—supply moves from S1 to S2. The equilibrium price of gasoline was $2.50/gallon before the ethanol mandate and is $3.00/gallon after the ethanol mandate. The loss in social gain is shown by the red triangle—the artificially high price of gasoline means we are worse off by this amount. But ethanol regulations cause social losses in markets other than gasoline.

Figure 2.8

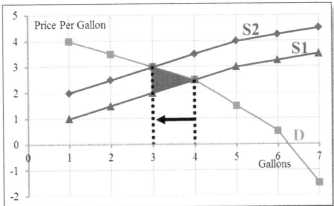

Because so much corn must be used in gasoline, there is a lower supply of corn for uses other than gasoline, which raises the price of corn in these uses. Since corn is used in cattle feed, the price of beef rises. Similarly, the price of corn sweeteners in candy and soft drinks rises, as do the prices of tortilla chips and corn-on-the-cob.

The subsidy gives wheat farmers an incentive to switch to growing corn. This reduces the supply of wheat, which raises the price of bread. We could show the losses from these sources in an illustration similar to the one above.

But even these costs are not the only ones we face. Even with the subsidies, other countries, especially in South America, can produce ethanol cheaper than we can in the US. Allowing trade in ethanol would bring down ethanol prices and gasoline prices. So the US restrict ethanol imports.

A final insanity concerns the mandate that companies use a billion gallons of cellulosic ethanol, made from grasses and other plants. Companies now only produce about 20,000 gallons of it, but they would need 50,000 times more to meet the mandate. The Environmental Protection Agency has fined oil refiners $10 million for not using a product which effectively does not exist.

Ethanol regulations are the result of special interest politics, driven not only by states which produce corn, but by politicians who are influenced by the corn lobby. At the ethanol mandate's inception, environmental groups also backed it, but, since then, their support has waned. Environmentalists value undeveloped land, but ethanol regulations cause more land to be developed for agriculture. In a good corn production year, one third of the crop goes into the gas tank. In a bad production year, half the crop goes into the gas tank.

Volume of Regulations

The graph below illustrates the number of pages of regulation the US government adds each year. They cover everything from how to take care of employees who herd goats, to how big a consumer's toilet tank can be, to which cleaners a janitor can use, to how to clean up a broken light bulb, to how a dishwasher should be made. Those who worked in feed stores during the last decade were surprised that the rat poison pellets they used had changed colors, from red to green, since the red dye caused cancer in rats and was, thus, cruel. Companies helping with the gulf oil spill were slowed because it is illegal to vacuum 90% oil from the water, separate most of it, and return water with only 1% oil—because it is illegal to put <u>any</u> oil in the gulf. In addition, some cleanup boats were from other countries and ran afoul of regulations which restricted foreign boats working in US waters, delaying them from helping for days. With so many and so varied regulations, no one can know if they are following the law.

Figure 2.9

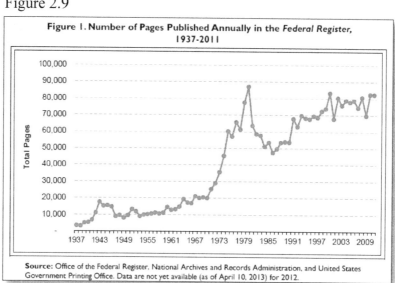

Figure 1. Number of Pages Published Annually in the Federal Register, 1937-2011
Total Pages
100,000
90,000
80,000
70,000
60,000
50,000
40,000
30,000
20,000
10,000
-
1937 1943 1949 1955 1961 1967 1973 1979 1985 1991 1997 2003 2009
Source: Office of the Federal Register, National Archives and Records Administration, and United States Government Printing Office. Data are not yet available (as of April 10, 2013) for 2012.

http://fas.org/sgp/crs/misc/R43056.pdf [reference]

The Other Side of Regulation—Why Some Businesses Like Some Regulations

Regulators who know about the industry which they regulate may be more effective. Hence, oil regulators often first worked in the oil business. Also, oil companies hire oil regulators in order to navigate the world of government mandates. Finally, current regulators can work best with industry cooperation, so they often develop cooperative relationships. This is true for all industries—banking, communications, insurance, aerospace, energy, etc. **Regulatory capture** occurs when regulators find it more advantageous to work to benefit some firms in their industries rather than to perform their oversight duties.

When regulatory agencies are captured, it is typically done by large firms resulting in regulations that favor large firms at the expense of small firms. This diminishes the market's advantages listed in the above section on knowledge in society, repeated here:

- Markets utilize the ingenuity of millions of minds.
- There are millions of small market experiments, each with low risk.
- In markets, there is competition to serve others.
- In markets, there are incentives to use resources efficiently.

Instead of millions of minds using their ingenuity, small competitors are disadvantaged and only a few regulators and heads of large firms may make the important decisions about production. In addition, we no longer have countless small, low risk experimenting entrepreneurs—we have a few huge firms and regulators that change the industry at a stroke, resulting in huge errors that destabilize the economy. There may be less competition to serve others and to use resources efficiently, as well.

Hence, regulation may be counter-productive. Each regulation claims to solve a problem. But, because of capture, many regulations end up serving the politically influential. So the antidote to "bad regulation" may not be "good regulation," since the process is often corrupted.

Rent seeking involves individuals expending resources to prosper, not by creating value, but by using the legal and regulatory systems. For instance, a firm can hire lobbyists to attempt to get the US Justice Department to sue a competitor. Or a firm can pay off legislators in return for tax dollars being spent on them or in return for passing laws restricting competitors' freedom.

Economist Bruce Yandle's experiences as a regulator led him to discover the **Bootleggers and Baptists** problem, an interesting form of rent seeking, because the rent seeker uses others to do his bidding. The bootleggers can only make a living if alcohol is *illegal*, since efficient legal production would put them out of business. So they depend on the Baptists, who also wish alcohol to be illegal, but for non-materialistic reasons, to protect them in the regulatory process. Hence, any special interest that wants to acquire taxpayer dollars or wants regulators to squash an opponent could profit from finding a group that supports their aims, but for a high-minded reason. http://www.econtalk.org/archives/2007/01/bruce_yandle_on.html [reference]

Yandle discovered the problem while reviewing regulations that would make manufacturing lawn mowers more expensive by mandating layers of safety equipment. He was surprised to find that a leading lawn mower manufacturer welcomed the regulations, since it would put all but a few manufacturers out of business, since only the large firms had sophisticated manufacturing processes to implement the safety features.

Yandle also observes that in the mid-90's tobacco lawsuit settlement, the US government mandated that any new cigarette manufacturer pay an up-front share of the settlement (millions of dollars to compensate for the future damages their product would cause). This provision insulated the existing tobacco companies from future competition, raising existing companies' profits. Further, the banning of flavored cigarettes in 2009 meant that many remaining small manufacturers would go out of business. The stated reason for the ban was that flavored cigarettes would attract underage smokers.

Also in 2009, congress enacted mandatory testing for lead in toys, children's clothing, and even children's books. No actual damage from any toy had been proven and only a handful of toys were found to contain lead. But large manufacturers seized on the ban as a way of putting small toy manufacturers out of business. Large toy makers were the bootleggers here, and the Baptists were those concerned with child safety. http://money.cnn.com/2009/01/14/smallbusiness/toy_law_threatens_small_companies.smb/ [reference]

In 1923 the US Supreme Court struck down a 1918 minimum wage law for women. Minimum wage laws are advocated as humanitarian help for low skilled people. Consider the effects of such a law today—setting the minimum wage that a woman can be paid at, perhaps, $15/hour. The regulators claimed that they were trying to improve conditions that women faced, but, in reality, the law was passed so that after World War I, women would be fired, opening jobs for male soldiers who were unemployed after returning from service in Europe. http://www.pbs.org/wnet/supremecourt/capitalism/landmark_adkins.html [reference]

In addition, unions have long been in favor of minimum wage laws because this makes it more expensive for union workers to be replaced with cheaper labor, since the minimum wage law raises the cost of non-union labor.

Wherever a new regulation is proposed, one must ask, "Who will gain from this?" Much of the time there is a financial incentive for one group to snatch value away from someone else in the economy, while, overall, destroying value.

Status Quo Minus Fallacy

The following statement contains a logical fallacy.

> Ten million children eat breakfast at McDonalds every day.
> Therefore, if there were no McDonalds, ten million children would go hungry.

Status quo minus **fallacy** is a particular variant of the status quo fallacy. It proposes that we consider the status quo, eliminate one element of it, and conjecture that this removed element will have only a direct effect which will never be compensated for. In reality, a parent who finds McDonalds closed will compensate by going somewhere else for breakfast, like Chic-fil-A. If McDonalds remains closed forever, in a market economy the unmet needs will cause existing firms to expand or new firms to arise to meet these needs—because it is profitable to do so.

As applied to regulation, those who suffer from the status quo minus fallacy think that if a regulation is removed that the only effect will be on the previously regulated behavior, so that a bad behavior will flourish and a good behavior will disappear.

Many who are in favor of making some drugs illegal assume that the only thing holding back consumption of the drug is the law. Many also assume that the crime problem that accompanies illegal drugs will increase if the substances are legalized. However, individuals have many other motivations for abstaining from illegal drugs—as witnessed by the fact that although alcohol is legal, not everyone is an alcoholic. Furthermore, much of the crime associated with illegal drugs has more to do with the "illegal" part than the "drugs" part. When alcohol prohibition was repealed, murders associated with alcohol manufacture and sale nearly vanished. http://www.cato.org/pubs/pas/pa-157.html [reference]

Here is another example of status quo minus thinking. *Child labor laws prevent twelve year olds from being hired out at hard labor by their parents. So if there were not child labor laws, twelve year olds would be hired out by their parents.* In reality, abolishing child labor laws would change almost nothing about the world. A few more bat boys would be hired at minor league games. http://www.nytimes.com/1993/05/28/us/batboy-is-called-out-by-labor-officials-who-vow-a-review.html [reference]. If a small number of twelve year olds were hired out for wages after repealing the law, then they would probably be from families who had difficulty feeding themselves. For these families, child labor laws mandate that children have more leisure and less food.

Minimum wage laws prevent employers from paying any employee a wage that is as low as the employer wishes—even $1/hour. So if there were no minimum wage law, employers would pay a wage as low as they want—even $1/hour. If the minimum wage were abolished, very little would change. First of all, of the 144 million workers in the country, 1.6 million earn the minimum wage—1.1% of workers. So minimum wage laws are not preventing many employers from paying low wages. If minimum wage laws were abolished, only those with extremely low skills would be paid less. However, it would be the case that some whose skill is so low that they cannot find employment at the minimum wage would then be hired at lower wages—mostly 16 and 17 year olds, whose unemployment rates are now at around 25%. Note that since young workers are the worst paid—3% of minimum wage workers are over 25 years old—college students are more likely to have been recently paid minimum wage, or know someone who is. http://www.bls.gov/cps/minwage2012.htm [reference]

THE LAW OF UNINTENDED CONSEQUENCES

Individual interaction is complex and individuals adjust to rules in ways that the rule makers do not anticipate. The **law of unintended consequences** is the warning that intervening in a complex system may create unanticipated and often undesirable outcomes. Individuals who adjust to interventions may not only weaken the intended results of the interventions, but sometimes cause the intervention to have the opposite of the intended effect. The following paragraphs give examples of the law.

Many advocate clean air regulation within the US to reduce the effect of man-made global warning. Proposed regulations would cause some resources to be used in an otherwise inefficient manner and cause other resources to remain idle. Due to global competition, firms may be forced to choose between bankruptcy in the US or profits abroad. As firms move production to other countries, such as China and India, where clean-air regulations are lower or non-existent, they will pollute even more than before the new regulations. Hence, US pollution laws that raise the cost of producing at home, actually increase global pollution. A law intended to reduce a particular global pollutant will likely increase it.

Seat belt laws are intended to save lives on the highway. But wearing a seat belt can change individual behavior. Suppose that a driver realizes that the seat belt is broken and will not protect from harm in an accident. The driver's only new incentive is to drive safer, since an accident will be more costly. But, said another way, wearing a seat belt encourages a driver to drive crazier, which increases the likelihood of an accident. Sam Peltzman, of the University of Chicago, discovered this effect and found that whenever seat belt laws were passed in a state, the number of accidents jumped sharply and the number of pedestrian deaths increased. Given that someone is in an accident, they are less likely to die if they are wearing a seat belt, but since they are more likely to be in an accident it is unclear whether seat belts, on balance, save lives or kill. In some places seat belts, although resulting in more accidents and pedestrian deaths, resulted in fewer deaths, overall. In other places the seat belt requirement resulted in more deaths, overall.

People with pre-existing conditions may have a more difficult time getting health insurance. The state, wanting more people to be insured, passes a law saying that an insurance provider cannot refuse someone because they have a pre-existing condition. Consider the effect on someone who is healthy. Health insurance may cost $5,000-$15,000 per year. A major reason to insure is to guard against *the big illness*, with medical bills that are far in excess of those amounts—$250,000 or $5 million, for instance. If one could not be refused due to a pre-existing condition, then those who do not have *the big illness* could save their yearly multi-thousand dollar premiums and would only insure if they did develop the big illness. This would mean that the only people who want to insure have *the big illness*. Thus, all insurance premiums would rise to hundreds of thousands or millions of dollars per year—likely destroying the market. When we begin by trying to help more people have health insurance, we may change incentives so that fewer people have health insurance.

THE NEWS MEDIA

Most of the traditional news media are often not equipped to deal with issues like these. They tell simple, surface stories and cannot see, like Bastiat, what lies below the surface—even if it is not very far below the surface. Examples include Bastiat's observation that hiring a government worker will reduce employment in agriculture, or that subsidizing the theater/entertainment industry results in the public having less food. Even those who understand simplify their message to get ratings from a public which rarely breaks its rationally ignorant habit.

The media is afflicted with status quo minus thinking. If forty-two million Americans use food stamps, then without food stamps they will starve. If there were no CAFE standards, then car companies would not make fuel efficient cars. If the state did not provide education, then there would be no education.

These simple stories imply a mythical government that is more knowledgeable than individuals and is able to move individuals about like chess men on a board, for the individuals' betterment. As Adam Smith, often called the father of modern economics, said in *The Theory of Moral Sentiments*,

> The man of system . . . is apt to be very wise in his own conceit; and is often so enamoured with the supposed beauty of his own ideal plan of government, that he cannot suffer the smallest deviation from any part of it . . . . He seems to imagine that he can arrange the different members of a great society with as much ease as the hand arranges the different pieces upon a chess-board. He does not consider that the pieces upon the chess-board have no other principle of motion besides that which the hand impresses upon them; but that, in the great chess-board of human society, every single piece has a principle of motion of its own, altogether different from that which the legislature might chuse to impress upon it. If [the government's wishes and society's wishes] coincide and act in the same direction, the game of human society will go on easily and harmoniously, and is very likely to be happy and successful. If they are opposite or different, the game will go on miserably, and the society must be at all times in the highest degree of disorder.
>
> *Smith*

About these calculated moves, Hayek tells us that no one knows how big the board is, what the pieces are, and how intricate the interlocking and changing rules are. But Hayek's version of spontaneous order tells us that individuals have the knowledge to navigate their sections of the board and to comprehend and adjust the rules. Bruce Yandle tells us that often the biggest pieces on the board are working through other pieces to influence the great government hand. The law of unintended consequences shows, time after time, that these economists have a point—the state's decision makers do not comprehend the game.

Further, the public choice school reminds us that the state is made up of people who are making decisions to make themselves better off—as you and I are. And although the state may produce good political theater, you and I are not their chief concern. They are playing the game to win for themselves, not for the pieces they sacrifice.

Value Creation Through Production

If a society could be made materially well off by having lots of dollars, then we could immediately solve all our problems by printing piles of dollars. But if you, and everyone around you, had $100 million in their bank accounts, you would demand $50,000 to mow a lawn and you would have to pay $1,000 to get someone to make you a sandwich. So societies with many dollars and nothing else are not well off.

Picture a society in which all the rocks lying around are gold and all the trees are covered with gold. No one would desire more gold. No one would want to find more gold. It would be worthless, except in the way that people today might pick up a pretty rock from the ground and show it to someone.

What makes gold valuable is its relative scarcity, a concept discussed in Chapter 1. But it is nonsensical to say that everyone would be materially well off if they possess lots of things that are relatively scarce—because then those things would not be relatively scarce.

Adam Smith, the father of modern economics, said, "the wealth of a country consists, not in its gold and silver only, but in its lands, houses, and consumable goods of all different kinds."

Money only makes transactions easier and stores value. Other than their uses in jewelry and industry, gold and silver are just means of exchanging value, storing value, and keeping track of prices, income, and wealth. Dollars have even fewer uses than gold and silver—except for keeping track of economic activity.

Smith says we are wealthy if we are able to consume valuable stuff. In order to consume something of value we must, first, create that value, and value is created in only two ways—through production and through trade. Economists often demonstrate these principles in a simplified economy, such as the book, *Robinson Crusoe*, or the movie, *Castaway*.

THE PRODUCTION PROCESS

Story: How He Could Help

Meg ran through the sand, yelling at Arn. "Stop! Where are you going?"

He turned his head and yelled back at her, still walking toward the surf. "For a swim."

She caught him just as their toes splashed in the foamy shallows, beside a stinking shark-like carcass. Leaning, hands on knees, she panted. Finally she said, "Why'd you leave the meeting?"

"Because I'd rather die quick than die slow. We made sure nobody knew where we were. That means we'll never be rescued. I'll swim out so far that I won't have the strength to swim back."

"It won't be as bad as you said back there. We have a few days food left, and stuff grows here—"

He snorted. "Stuff that's poison to us."

"Maybe not all of it," she said. "We haven't tried to eat everything."

"Sal tried, and you saw how he died." Arn spat into the ocean. "Do you want to die like that?"

She shrugged. "Sal had one success and one failure. Maybe it's our only failure. I've already used the knife to strip slats off trees. I think if I boil them I can weave them and maybe make panels to build huts—get us off the ground and away from the crawlies. We're just getting started."

He turned, so the wind would blow his hair out of his eyes instead of into them. "Pirates like us don't 'just get started,'—that's for colonists."

Meg put a hand on his shoulder. "And we look out for each other. We need everybody."

He scoffed. "I'm communications and surveillance. With no power, what can I do to help?"

She shook her head. "You'll have to figure that out as we go."

He waded into the breakers, past their downed space ship. She screamed at him, "If you drown and the tide brings you in, you'll be a few meals for us. You can help with that, if the fish don't eat you first." He kept walking.

She called, "If you change your mind, you know where we'll be."

How He Could Help gets back to basics. We have resources and knowledge, and hope to find more resources and knowledge to improve our lives—one way is through production.

The **production process** turns inputs into consumable outputs. The **consumable outputs** are goods and services.

The **resources/inputs** are:

Table 3.1

Resources/Inputs	Definition	Cost
Natural Resources/land	tangible, but not produced by anyone	Rent
Labor	physical and mental talents, applied to production	Wage
Capital	produced means of production	Interest
Entrepreneurship	risk taking/risk bearing and innovation	Profit

Chapter 1 discussed production briefly, developing the marginal cost curve and tying its shape to the law of diminishing returns, which says that as we add workers to a production process with some fixed inputs (like factory space), eventually we cannot find ways to utilize them in a highly productive way—as in the second Ramona's restaurant story, *The Worst Thing*. We also tied the marginal cost curve to the optimal arrangement principal—individuals give up the least valuable alternatives first, but that means that as they continue to produce they must give up more valuable alternatives, so costs rise as more is produced.

In a modern economy production involves many stages. We could not list all the resources necessary to produce an iPhone, for instance, especially if we wish to discuss a working iPhone with electricity and towers. No living person could build an iPhone. It takes hundreds of thousands of individuals, designing the phone, mining the materials, building the mining equipment, manufacturing fuel for the equipment, drilling for fuel for the equipment, designing the factory to make each component of the phone, running the factory to manufacture each phone component, and so on.

It takes a huge economic engine, connected by the price system, which conveys the necessary information about the scarcity of each resource, the preferences of consumers, and provides incentives for working together. Apple does not control this engine. The engine is the spontaneous order of the world economy.

You can find a simpler 1850's example in Bastiat's essay, but even so, the process is not elementary. Read Bastiat's Chapter 6 (Middlemen). http://www.econlib.org/library/Bastiat/basEss1.html [essential]

Thinking Exercise 3.1: Inputs and Outputs

- Find one of each of the types of resources in *How He Could Help*.
- Find one of each of the types of resources in Bastiat's Chapter 6, Middlemen.
- How many stages of the production process for a coat does Bastiat list? Are there any stages he does not list?
- Who are the middlemen in Bastiat's coat example? Who are not middlemen in Bastiat's coat example?
- What does Bastiat say will keep grain profits under control?
- How much does Bastiat claim profits are?
- What does Bastiat say will keep costs of grain shipment under control?
- Bastiat says that some people think government would have lower costs of grain deliveries. What reason does Bastiat give for that thinking?
- Does Bastiat agree? Why or why not?
- Why does Bastiat say that grain will first go to the places that need it most?
- What does Bastiat say about the socialists' views about organization vs. market organization?
- Are there any highly profitable companies that act as middlemen today?
- Which middlemen are unpopular today?

It is easier to list those who are not middlemen in the production process than to list all those who are, because there are so many. People often simplify this problem and say that a middleman is one who does not change the value of the product that the final consumer uses. But if middlemen had no effect on the value, no one would pay them—and value is defined as willingness to sacrifice, or pay.

TECHNOLOGY

Technology is the way that inputs are combined to produce output. We often think of technology as being associated with computers and satellites, but our definition is simpler than that, including other, basic things.

The basic process for producing eggs is that food and water go in the chicken's front end and eggs come out the back end. However, according to economist Russell Roberts, in the US, the average chicken lays 350 eggs/year, while the average chicken in the developing world lays about 50 eggs/year. US chickens are much more productive because of the use of technologies that have nothing to do with lasers or quantum entanglement. It has to do with what the chickens are fed, how the chickens are cared for, and chicken house automation. http://www.econtalk.org/archives/2007/02/lucas_on_growth.html [reference] (skip to 18:46).

Karl Marx thought that technology caused unemployment. He was right in one sense, but was wrong in the most meaningful sense, as the next story illustrates.

Story: Out of Work

When Georg tapped Arn on the shoulder, Arn whirled around and drew back a chunk of glassy white rock.

Georg shot out a hand out to block a blow. "Easy, guy. Armed and dangerous."

Arn relaxed and whispered, "What do you want?"

Georg saw Meg and Cinda thirty yards away through the foliage. Arn had been watching them. Georg said, "I'm trying to trap and pen some of those heavy mammals in the center of the island, so we'll have a dependable supply of meat close by, rather than taking everyone out to hunt every time we want another one. Looks like you're not doing anything but watching Meg and Cinda, so come help me."

Arn nodded, turning to look at the two women again. "They're making a ladder. They've been at it for three days—Cinda's not fishing and Meg's not helping pick oilnuts. They saved food beforehand and they're eating less while they're making it. They're stripping bark, making cords, whittling at poles. It's going to put me out of my job, climbing for bluefruits."

"Dammit, Arn," Georg said, looking at the chunk of rock in Arn's hand. "You were planning to kill them for making a ladder."

"No, no. I wasn't going to kill them. It's just that I'm the only one who can climb the crazy trees on this planet, but with a ladder, anybody can pick bluefruits. So I . . . I . . . ."

Georg rolled his eyes. "Please don't kill anybody for finding ways to get more food. We need better food, better clothes, better shelter—better everything."

"I wasn't going to—"

"Tell you what. When we have everything we ever need, at our disposal, you'll be out of a job." Georg motioned for Arn to follow him. "Until then, I could use some help penning those critters. Maybe if we can convince the critters to cook and serve themselves to us, we'll all be out of jobs. Isn't that exactly what we want?"

❁❁❁❁❁❁❁❁❁❁❁❁❁❁❁❁❁❁❁❁❁❁❁❁❁❁❁❁❁❁❁

We do not really want work. If we did, we would pay our employer to assign work to us—our employer would not have to pay us to do work. We want the goods and services that work provides. And, if we can get those things with less effort or get more of them for the same effort, we are better off. As resources are released from producing one good, they become available to produce others, making us wealthier.

Milton Friedman, one of the greatest economists of the last century, told a story about his visit to India. His guide took him to a site where workers were digging a canal with shovels. When Friedman asked why they didn't use bulldozers the guide said that the canal was a jobs program and bulldozers would eliminate jobs. Friedman replied that he thought their goal was to build a canal. He told the guide that if they were just trying to create jobs, the workers should use spoons.

http://www.realclearpolitics.com/2011/06/22/why_technology_doesn039t_destroy_jobs_257909.html [reference]

The idea that jobs are valuable, whether or not the labor's production adds value, is called **make work fallacy**. The public and the media suffer under the great delusion of make work fallacy.

PRODUCTION POSSIBLITIES FRONTIER

The production possibilities frontier (PPF) model is a simplified way of understanding the production tradeoffs that are made in an economy. The PPF model assumes three things:

- Only two goods are produced over some time period.
- Some fixed amount of resources is used.
- A given technology is used.

Suppose the only two goods produced on the island are fish and coconuts and that the population divides its labor and other resources between the two goods. If they produce only fish, there is some maximum amount they can produce, and the same works for coconuts. Suppose these maximum amounts are 5 fish and 25 coconuts. We can illustrate this by the following graph.

Figure 3.1

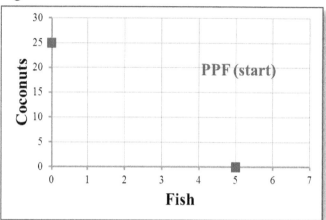

One choice that the islanders can make has 0 fish and 25 coconuts. Another choice has 5 fish and 0 coconuts. They make these choices by using labor and other resources to either catch fish or gather coconuts. *If all coconut trees were the same and all fishing spots and times of the day for fishing were the same and all laborers were the same*, then they would be able to shift resources so that there was a fixed proportion—for every fish caught they would have to give up 5 coconuts. That would say the cost of a fish is 5 coconuts—and the cost of a coconut is 1/5 of a fish. Their choices would lie along this line, which has a slope equal to -5.

Figure 3.2

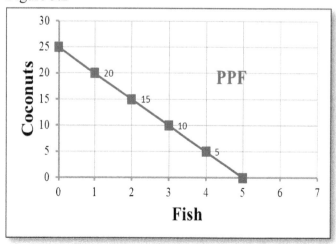

But some coconuts are on the ground, and some are in nearby trees, and some are in low trees, and some people are good at gathering coconuts and some people are good at fishing. So if we begin by only producing coconuts, then start to catch fish—giving up some coconuts—we arrange things to give up the least amount of coconuts per fish. We do this by continuing to gather coconuts on the ground, but giving up hard-to-get-to coconuts, and by using our best coconut gatherers for coconuts and our best fishermen for fishing. This, again, is simply the principle of optimal arrangement (POA). The result is the same as in Chapter 1—as we catch more fish the cost of another fish rises. Remember the cost of fish is how many coconuts must be sacrificed. *Applying the POA to production of two goods where resources are not all the same*, results in the **law of increasing opportunity cost** (LIOC)—as more of one good is produced, the opportunity cost of producing a unit of that good rises, in terms of the other good which must be sacrificed.

The LIOC does not only work in producing fish and coconuts. A particular resource has different productivities when applied to manufacture of health care, vs. phones vs. construction. So the POA will be efficiently applied, which means the LIOC applies to tradeoffs between all real world goods.

But when one is trading off two goods, the law of increasing opportunity costs does not mean that the PPF slopes upward, as the marginal cost curve does. Remember the cost of one good in terms of another is the slope. So as we catch more fish, the slope of the PPF increases, like this.

Figure 3.3

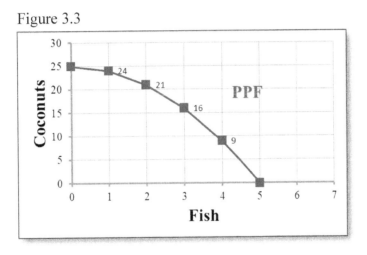

If we switch the axes of the PPF, we get the same result. The slope—the opportunity cost of gathering another coconut—falls. So the PPF is bowed outward.

Many wish to know which combination of fish and coconuts is the best. But this information cannot be found on the PPF because it only shows *possibilities*—not preferences. Some people like coconuts more and some like fish more. To answer the question, "which is the best," we'd have to know people's preferences for the two goods—fish and coconuts, in our example.

A market economy answers the question of how much to produce, as in Chapter 1, through the spontaneous order of the market. North Korea mostly answers these questions by authoritarian choice, discussed in Chapter 2. In the US economy some decisions are made in markets, some decisions are the authoritarian choices of elected representatives, and a minute number of decisions are made by democratic choice.

The PPF is a simplified model, since it only has two goods. If there were more goods, many of the principles we have discussed would remain the same. The only real difference is that to increase production of fish, one could give up some coconuts and some of another good, like pineapples. The chapter begins on the island to avoid pre-conceived notions that money is the important thing in production. As in the Adam Smith quote, wealth is not really money. Wealth is about having valuable stuff.

But now that we have a foundation, we can consider the usual economic tradeoffs like food and health care. As a nation, we can have more health care, but as we devote resources to health care, we devote less to food. If we consider all the other goods, not just two, then to have more health care, we must give up something—food, clothing, shelter, transportation, education, and the like. So health care is great, but an authoritarian economy might give up too many houses to have more health care, or could give up too much health care to build too many houses, because we have no guarantee that authoritarian decisions will reflect the values of those taking part in the economy. A market economy would never do these things, since all choices are based on value. As long as another house is more valuable than another MRI machine, someone will pay more for another house, and vice versa.

On the PPF, the islanders could not have 5 fish *and* 20 coconuts. They could have 1 fish and 10 coconuts—but only by letting some of their resources be unemployed. In the graph below, choices in the green region are not yet possible. Choices in the blue region are attainable, but are inefficient—wasted or unemployed resources. Hence, the PPF is exactly what the name says. It is the frontier of all the combinations that are possible to produce.

Figure 3.4

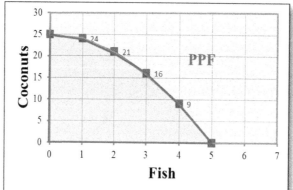

Choices in the green region may one day be attainable if the economy has more resources, better resources, or better technologies. If this happens, we say that **economic growth** has occurred—an expansion of an economy's productive capabilities. Economic growth is illustrated in the graph below by the original frontier shifting outward, so that more choices are possible to produce.

Figure 3.5

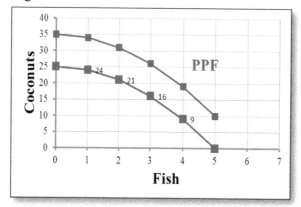

Thinking Exercise 3.2

- List the 4 types or resources that we use in production.
- For each type of resource, list all the reasons the resource could increase.
- List any policies that might help the resource to increase.
- List any policies that we now use that might cause the resource to decrease.
- List any policies that might help or harm technology.
- In each answer, please remember the lessons you have learned so far from Bastiat—consider the seen and the unseen, as Bastiat has developed those concepts.

INCOME AND WEALTH DETERMINANTS

For individuals and for entire economies, income and wealth depend on three things:

- Quantity of resources,
- Quality of resources, and
- Freedom to use those resources.

There are many ins and outs, qualifiers and exceptions, but these are the basics. Individuals upgrade their labor by education and training—developing their **human capital**. Individuals can save some of their income and build their physical capital as well—buying "the produced means of production" from someone else. With the freedom to do these things in a market economy, those who can provide value are able consume some of that value. Those who cannot provide as much value have less to consume. This gives incentives for greater creation of value, that is, for providing greater market service to each other. Adam Smith said,

> It is not from the benevolence of the butcher, the brewer, or the baker, that we expect our dinner, but from their regard to their own interest. We address ourselves, not to their humanity but to their self-love, and never talk to them of our own necessities but of their advantages.
> *Smith*

And as we serve one another, seeking to be well off, materially, we fit together in a spontaneous order that almost seems planned, but is, in reality, better than what any individual could plan. On the topic, Smith also said,

> [H]e intends only his own gain, and he is . . . led by an **invisible hand** to promote an end which was no part of his intention . . . . By pursuing his own interest he frequently promotes that of the society more effectually than when he really intends to promote it. I have never known much good done by those who affected to trade for the public good.
> *Smith*

That is, those who are just trying to help themselves often help others more than when they are actually trying to help others. In the Chapter 1 story, *The Best Thing*, Gregg can be of the most value to society by bidding out his services. Those who value his services the most will sacrifice the most to acquire his services.

Value Creation Through Trade

Cinda dug her toes into the sand of the circle and said, "Anything for the future? If not, we're adjourned—the fire is burning low."

Arn leaned back against a tree and said, "I'm not catching pigs anymore."

"They're not pigs. They're—" Georg started.

"They're delicious," Cinda broke in. "And we won't be able to keep eating one per week if you stop. You're our best hunter and they've just started breeding in Georg's pen."

Arn spat into the fire. "Running around like that is hard on my feet. I don't get enough pig to pay for my trouble. I'd rather climb."

Meg said, "We don't need another climber, since we made the ladder."

"The stupid ladder," Arn said. "Then I'll fish—I did that for a week and liked it."

Jyn lolled her head on Sam's shoulder and said, "We got that covered. I find 'em and Sam nets."

"Speaking of fishing," Meg said. "I want to build nets over the mouth of the lagoon. We can pen fish just like the pigs—I know, Georg, they're not pigs."

Cinda cocked her head. "That's a lot of net."

"It'll take about six months if all eight of us work together. I'll do weekly repairs after that."

Arn said, "So we'll be going hungry for that long to make the thing. Count me out."

Meg said, "But then we could catch the day's fish in ten minutes and Jyn and Sam could do something else—we always need more oilnuts."

Cinda said, "We're not a dictatorship, so anybody that wants to give time to net building is welcome to. You can agree on how to split up the fish from it. Anybody?"

Four hands raised. Meg sighed. "So a year of hunger for four of us," All hands went down.

Arn chuckled. "If we had fifty people eating fish it would be worth it—only a month of hunger with fifty net weavers." He sighed. "I think I'll just gather oilnuts. Georg can catch pigs."

Cinda waved a hand. "Whatever works. That is, whatever gets Arn to work."

Trade occurs when goods, services, or resources are exchanged, sometimes using money as a medium of exchange. Trade without money is called **barter**. With money the concept of "buyer" and "seller" are well defined. Almost everyone regularly buys and sells—selling labor and buying goods and services. When people trade voluntarily, they do so to make themselves better off.

The end of Chapter 1 discussed the social gain that comes from producing and trading goods in markets. The social gains to sellers and buyers underlie all discussion of trade. One thing that the social gain model points out is that while Walmart gains from selling a Blu-Ray player to me, I also gain because it is almost certain that I did not have to pay the maximum I was willing to pay for it. Many people look at the direction that money goes in a trade and, not understanding what Adam Smith said about well-being, wrongly conclude that the person who ended up with the money has gained and the person who ended up paying has lost.

The incentive to trade comes from three motivations—people differ in tastes, people differ in abilities, and more highly populated markets give rise to better use of resources though specialization.

TRADE BASED ON TASTES

Thinking Exercise 4.1: Chocolate

You won a door prize, which has six different types of candy bar, and your friend won an identical prize. But you value the bars differently than each other.

- What do those numbers mean? That is, for you the Snickers bar has 0.7 value—but 0.7 what?
- What is the total value of your prize?
- Find one trade that makes both of you better off. Find more such trades.
- What is the total value of the bars after the trades you just identified?
- Where did this value come from?

Table 4.1

Bar	Your Value	Friend's Value
Snickers	0.7	0.5
Twix	0.6	0.4
Almond Joy	0.2	0.6
3 Musketeers	0.3	0.2
Butterfinger	0.5	0.7
Baby Ruth	0.4	0.9

Sometimes we trade because we like one thing more than another, or because we dislike something less than something else. For instance, even if the wage is the same for two jobs, you may prefer to work at one job more than at the other.

TRADE BASED ON THE DIVISION OF LABOR/EXTENT OF THE MARKET

Adam Smith begins his 1776 masterpiece, *The Wealth of Nations*, with an example of a factory that makes pins used in sewing. He describes the process in detail, observing how the laborers are specialists in one particular job and how they use specialized equipment in production. He concludes with the following:

Those ten persons, therefore, could make among them upwards of forty-eight thousand pins in a day. Each person, therefore, making a tenth part of forty-eight thousand pins, might be considered as making four thousand eight hundred pins in a day. But if they had all wrought separately and independently, and without any of them having been educated to this peculiar business, they certainly could not each of them have made twenty, perhaps not one pin in a day . . . .

Smith

The title to Chapter 3 of *The Wealth of Nations* is "The Division of Labour is Limited by the Extent of the Market." Here is what Smith means. As discussed in Chapter 2, no one person knows how to make an iPod, and certainly no one has all the skills to make an iPod. In fact, no one person knows how to make a pencil (http://www.econlib.org/library/Essays/rdPncl1.html) [reference]. They could describe the final process of putting it together, but few could do even that job, much less manufacture an eraser, mine graphite, obtain chemicals for paint, drill a hole through such a small wood strip. Millions of people trade with each other to make these goods. *But if only <u>one person</u> wanted to own a pencil or an iPod, it would not be profitable to do all the trading necessary to make them.* It is only efficient to engage in all the trades necessary to make these goods if the markets for pencils and iPods are so big that millions of units are desired.

A great deal of economic progress had to wait until cities were founded and grew. As that happened, it made sense to have larger scale production that took advantage of the division of labor in lowering costs, which freed up labor to do other useful things, further advancing the economy. The process continues today, to the point that it is cheaper to make pins in huge factories in China and pay to ship some to Guam, rather than produce them on Guam.

Today, "market" is less a geographical term than it was before. It does not matter how many people own Google Glasses in one town for a developer to specialize in apps. It matters how many people around the world own them.

TRADE BASED ON ABILITIES

Individuals have different abilities that they offer to the market as labor. Land and entrepreneurship is specialized, as well. Just as one person would make a better writer than engineer, one region would be a better place to mine copper than to grow oranges. Adam Smith got so much of economic theory right, but he missed a fine distinction with regard to trade based on abilities. It took David Ricardo, writing about fifty years after Smith's *Wealth of Nations* to make this distinction.

Table 4.2

	Arn	Meg
Fish	1 lb	1 lb
Grapes	3 pints	5 pints

Suppose Arn can catch 1 pound of fish in the same time he can pick 3 pints of grapes. Meg can catch 1 pound of fish in the same time she can pick 5 pints of grapes. Even though Meg is at least as good at producing both goods, Arn and Meg can still trade profitably. Here is a trade. Meg picks 4 pints of grapes and trades them to Arn for 1 pound of fish. Meg works less than she would have to in order to catch the pound of fish. And Arn catches the fish, sacrificing the time it would take to pick 3 pints of grapes—but he gets 4 pints of grapes.

The problem could have, just as easily, said Meg can catch 2 fish in the same amount of time that she could gather 10 grapes—this would simplify to 1 for 5, though. This simplification allows the logic of the solution to be extended to tables with any numbers. One would just have to pick one of the two products and adjust the amounts proportionally.

An individual has a **comparative advantage** at producing a good if he or she has a lower opportunity cost of producing the good, in terms of other goods sacrificed. Differences in abilities of individuals or of other resources give rise to comparative advantage.

In our example, Arn has the lowest cost of catching a fish in terms of the grapes he gives up, so Arn has a **comparative advantage** in fishing. Similarly, Meg has a comparative advantage in picking grapes. She gives up 1/5 of a pound of fish for each pint, whereas Arn gives up 1/3 of a pound of fish for each pint—Arn gives up more fish for each pound of grapes.

An individual can trade off one good for another internally, by putting their labor into one good, taking it away from another good. But an individual can also trade off one good for another externally by first producing the good, then trading it for a good that someone else has produced. If the external cost of trading for a good is lower than the internal cost of producing the good, then trade is advantageous.

SUMMING UP TRADE

Trade comes from three motivations—differences in tastes, abilities, and the expansion of the extent of the market. These motivations all form a part of the spontaneous order of the market economy. No one has to order people around with regard to trade, because they have an internal motivation—they wish to make themselves better off.

Trade is limited by transactions costs. **Transactions costs** arise due to the sacrifice that must be made to search out, negotiate, and complete an exchange. If these costs are too high, then trades that we have looked at previously in these examples might not take place.

We should also remember that we not only trade goods and services. We also trade resources—about 70% of imports are used to make other goods. Less expensive resources means that the supply of the goods that producers make rises, lowering costs and resulting in more being sold, expanding value for consumers and producers. The graph below shows the increase in supply.

Figure 4.1

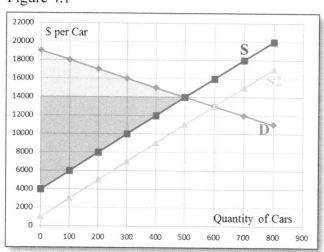

Because supply increases, prices fall and more is sold, expanding the consumer gain (blue) and the producer gain (red).

Figure 4.2

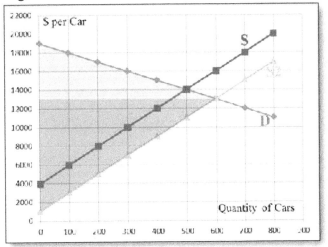

Comparing the two, society's gain—some for the producer and some for the consumer—has increased from the original consumer gain (blue) and original producer gain (red) by the green area.

Figure 4.3

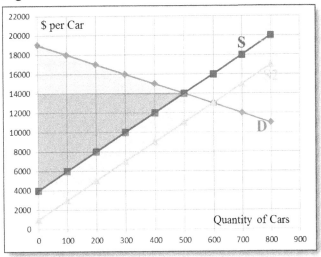

Thinking Exercise 4.3: Not Pigs and Not Nets

In the story above, find the examples of the following:

- Trade based on tastes
- Trade based on abilities
- Trade expansion due to the expansion of the market
- Transactions costs

TRADE AND MONEY

This chapter has avoided the idea of money in trade because money misleads. Recall, we are really only interested in having goods, now and later, not in pieces of paper or in bits and bytes. But the world falsely equates money to wellbeing. To understand that language, we must overlay our ideas onto the real economy.

The Balance of Trade and the Balance of Payments

In The *Wealth of Nations*, Smith thoroughly refuted mercantilism. But 250 years later, mercantilism is still alive in the news media and in the "wisdom" of the common man. Mercantilism is aimed at keeping as much money in the country as possible—not letting it escape. So to mercantilists, importing is bad and exporting is good. Mercantilists are obsessed with the **balance of trade**, the dollar value of exported goods and services minus the dollar value of imported goods and services—they think that nations become wealthy by having the highest possible positive balance. A positive balance of trade is called a **trade surplus**, while a negative balance of trade is called a **trade deficit**.

Bastiat humorously refuted proposals in the French parliament to legislate positive balances of trade. He describes himself as making the following transactions.

- I was at Bordeaux. I had a cask of wine which was worth 50 francs; I sent it to Liverpool, and the [French] custom house noted on its records an export of 50 francs.

- At Liverpool the wine was sold for 70 francs. My representative converted the 70 francs into coal, which was found to be worth 90 francs on the market at Bordeaux. The customhouse hastened to record an import of 90 francs.

- Balance of trade, or the excess of imports over exports: 40 francs.[deficit]

- These 40 francs, I have always believed, putting my trust in my books, I had gained. But [a mercantilist politician] tells me that I have lost them, and that France has lost them in my person.

- A few days after my transaction . . . the price of wine fell at Bordeaux and rose at Liverpool; so that if I had not been so hasty, I could have bought at 40 francs and sold at 100 francs. I truly believed that on such a basis my profit would have been greater. But I learn from [the mercantilist politician] that . . . the loss that would have been more ruinous.

- My second transaction had a very different result. I had had some truffles... which cost me 100 francs; they were destined for two distinguished English cabinet ministers for a very high price, which I proposed to turn into pounds sterling.

- The ship that carried them off sank on its departure. The [French] customs officer, who had noted on this occasion an export of 100 francs, never had any re-import to enter in this case.

- Hence, [the mercantilist politician] would say, France gained 100 francs; for it was, in fact, by this sum that the export, thanks to the shipwreck, exceeded the import.

http://www.econlib.org/library/Bastiat/basEss13.html [essential]

Note that, in this discussion, for every flow of money there is also a matching flow of goods. When someone in France gains money, someone else in France is not consuming the exported goods. If we consider the goods flows and the money flows, each transaction nets out. If we only consider the goods flows, Bastiat's first transaction turns wine into more valuable coal. Bastiat's example also points out that if we count it a loss for an American car dealership when a car is imported from Germany, we must also count it a profit for an American importer, whose employees are also thankful for the import.

Mercantilists, who worry about the drain of money from an economy, only look at what is called **the current account**—the monetary value of the flow of goods and services. But, when the US imports oil from Canada, what do Canadians do with those US dollars? Just as Walmart in the US will not accept Canadian dollars, in Canada they do not accept US dollars. Ultimately those dollars either purchase US goods and services—resulting in an eventual balance of the current account—or they purchase financial instruments, the stocks and bonds of US companies and/or governments, which adds to the monetary value of **the capital account**. Hence, the two accounts always offset each other, so the **balance of payments**, the sum of the current account and the capital account, is always zero. If we import more goods than we export, foreigners must be investing in our companies or our government, which we consider a good thing.

Further, if mercantilism were good for the US, mercantilism would be good for Georgia—to not import from any other state—and good for the county, and good for the city, and good for the people on your street, and even good for your household. If we personalize the balance of trade, we may find that a professor has a huge positive balance with the state of Georgia and a huge negative balance with Walmart. He could improve his mercantilist position by refusing to shop anywhere—by hoarding cash, growing his own food, building his own house, not using a phone or cable TV. That is, if he wishes to have a favorable balance of trade he should work all the time and live in the Stone Age. He may starve, sitting on his huge pile of money. This is the mercantilist's prescription for wealth. It ignores what Adam Smith said—that the true wealth of a nation lies in possessing goods and services.

Story: The New Country

After the ground stopped shaking, Cinda stood with Meg and Arn on one side of the ditch, formed where the land had receded along the middle of the island, looking across the ankle-deep six-foot wide trench of seawater, at the others.

On the other side, Ed said, "A miracle nobody was hurt."

Arn sat on the ground. "It will be worse, now that there's two islands, Ed. I'm unemployed since the oilnuts are on your island. I'll climb to gather coconuts on our island, since the ladder is on your side, too. And I'll miss Georg's pigs."

"They're not pigs," Georg said.

Ed said, "It'll be tough for everybody because we can't all work together anymore. You'll be hungrier, with less hands to pitch in and work, but your island has Meg, so you'll have the woven shelters and the knife."

Georg rolled his eyes. Cinda put her head on Meg's shoulder and laughed. "Idiots."

✧✧✧✧✧✧✧✧✧✧✧✧✧✧✧✧✧✧✧✧✧✧✧✧✧✧✧✧✧

The mercantilism of the populace can be self-contradictory. A well-known media figure recently said that oil imports harm the US by sending money overseas, but he also says that oil exports harm the US by sending oil overseas in return for money. Few well-known media figures understand economics—or logic.

Story: The Color of Lawns

Biff said, "Diamond Point will never be as rich as Arrowwood unless we stop paying poor people to do our landscaping!" Ted agreed. They convinced the homeowner's association, overriding Chuck's objection that hiring landscapers was charitable to the poor. So Diamond Point would only hire residents.

Here's what happened.

Ted said, "Biff, I gave up $40 K in legal work this year because I was landscaping. Would you do my landscaping next year for $10 K?"

Biff shook his head. "No way. I think I'm down $30 K from last year. I would hire you, but your lawn sucks. Man, take some time off to figure out how to balance your pH."

"Time off? Can't I hire somebody to just to balance my pH? That's not really lawn work, and I can't afford more time off."

Biff rolled his eyes. "Read last year's agreement, man. We agreed not to hire out for <u>any</u> landscaping services. I hired a Diamond Point accountant to spread lime for $2 K. He said that getting a landscaping education cost him $60 K worth of business, so he had to charge so much."

Ted said, "Maybe Chuck was right. Maybe we should be charitable to the folks in Jones Ford and hire them. That subdivision is so poor that they're full of free trade economists."

Exchange Rates

Since there are different monetary systems, international trade requires the buying and selling of each country's currency. If someone in Mexico wanted to buy your band's music, you would want to be paid in dollars, so someone would have to use pesos to purchase dollars, whether you or they—the usual arrangement is that the buyer must have the correct currency. The price of one country's currency in terms of another country's currency is the **exchange rate**. As with every other price, the exchange rate depends on the supply and demand for each currency.

Below is the market for dollars, in terms of pesos. If one is buying and selling dollars, then the good on the horizontal axis is dollars and the price on the vertical axis is given in pesos per dollar.

Figure 4.4

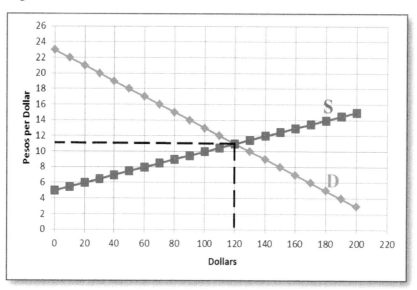

The demand for dollars is determined by:

- How many US goods, services, and financial instruments the rest of the world wants, and
- Whether people expect the dollar to gain or lose value in the future—in terms of other currencies.

The supply of dollars is determined by:

- How many of the rest of the world's good, services, and financial instruments that people holding dollars wish to have,
- Whether people expect the dollar to gain or lose value—in terms of other currencies, and
- The central bank—the US Federal Reserve Bank (the Fed) creating or destroying money.

This graph shows that currently 11 pesos will purchase $1. This means that 1 peso is worth 1/11th of $1, which is about 9 cents.

Suppose that next month it takes 13 pesos to purchase $1—the peso will be worth 7.7 cents—that is, the dollar will be more valuable in terms of pesos. The **dollar has appreciated**—gained in value, compared to the peso.

Thinking Exercise 4.4: Appreciation Blues

Suppose this month the price of $1 is 11 pesos and next month the price of $1 is 13 pesos.
- If you sell your album for $10, how much does a Mexican pay this month for it?
- How much does a Mexican pay for it next month?
- Is it easier to sell your album this month or next month?

You are buying furniture from Mexico for $200 and selling it in the US for $250. If your sales price remains the same, and the Mexican exporter does not change the price you pay in pesos,
- How much profit do you make this month?
- How much profit do you make next month?

An appreciation of the dollar makes it less profitable to export and more profitable to import. A depreciation of the dollar has the opposite effect. People who work in a US industry that depends on exports would prefer a weak dollar. People who work in a US industry that uses many foreign resources prefer a strong dollar. People who buy gasoline in the US prefer a strong dollar.

At times people in the US have worried about another country's exports "taking over the world." In the 1980s, the perceived enemy was Japan. The reason their exports were so strong was because their goods were higher quality than US goods. But with Japan, as with other exporters, the more they export, the more of their currency, yen, people need. People now fear China, most of all.

Suppose Mexico feared imports from the US—the world's largest economy. As Mexicans import more US goods, the demand for the dollar increases, so its price increases, as seen below. This appreciation makes the prices of US exported goods rise, making the US less competitive.

Figure 4.5

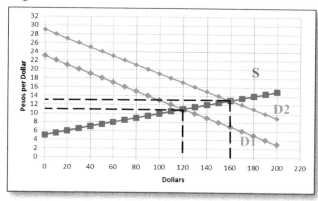

One way that nations try to cheat these economic relationships is through the use of the central bank—in the case of the US, the Federal Reserve System (the Fed). Besides the dollars from those who have goods and financial instruments to sell, the Fed can artificially push dollars into the economy, increasing the money supply, by purchasing financial instruments. Traditionally, the Fed buys bonds from the public—bonds that the US government sold to the public to finance US government spending. As the money supply rises, dollars are easier to find, so their price falls—that is, the dollar depreciates, as shown below.

Figure 4.6

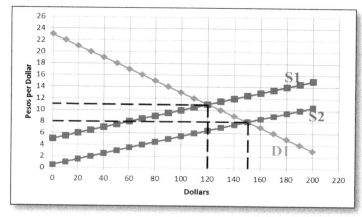

But, as previously stated, this hurts industries that import, including those who import resources such as steel and oil. As these prices rise, industries that use these resources shrink and lose jobs.

The economy is complex, so these actions cause unexpected results. For instance, the largest importer of steel in the US is not the auto or construction industries, though higher steel imports would hurt them, too. The largest importer of steel is the steel industry. Companies in the US buy unfinished steel from other countries, finish it in the US and sell it. So increases in the price foreign steel, through depreciation of the dollar, even hurt the steel industry. Further, as the price of wheat sold to Italy falls due to Fed actions, the price of spaghetti that Italians make from the wheat and export to the US also falls, causing problems for US pasta makers.

Central banks never try to enhance imports by lowering the money supply, though the most respected economists, including Smith, Ricardo, Bastiat, Hayek, and Friedman have affirmed that both voluntary imports and exports increase economic wellbeing. Even at high levels of state decision making, where policy makers are supposed to know better, mercantilist instincts are strong. In spite of simple, powerful arguments like Bastiat's, earlier in the chapter, many still incorrectly think, "Exports—good. Imports—bad."

State Restraint of Trade

Read Bastiat's Chapter 7: Restraint of Trade http://www.econlib.org/library/Bastiat/basEss1.html
[essential] *(Be sure to read about Bastiat's reference to the French hat, which he calls, "an article of millinery," in the appendix to this chapter.)*

- Who is Mr. Protectionist's enemy?
- Why does Bastiat use the phrase "law factory?"
- How does Mr. Protectionist say that the law will benefit the nation?
- If the law is passed, what actions does the state take to help Mr. Protectionist?
- Does the protectionist law merely take dollars from the consumer and hand them to the producer? Explain where the losses are.
- Which is worse, legal plunder or illegal plunder? Why?
- In today's society, who loses from trade? How do we know? Who wins?

Modern day mercantilists are sometimes called "**protectionists**." The state restrains trade through a few means.

- **Tariffs**—taxes on imports, sometimes more than 100% of the import's price.
- **Quotas**—restrictions on the quantity of imports that citizens can purchase.
- **Subsidies**—paying domestic firms to produce. Unless foreign governments retaliate, foreign industries can't compete.
- **Export subsidies**—paying domestic firms for each unit they export.
- **Domestic content restrictions**—laws that say a product made in the country must be primarily made using resources from the country.
- **Anti-competitive manufacturing specifications**—requiring that a particular imported product be manufactured with inputs that are difficult to acquire except in the importing country.

Above, under "Summing Up Trade," the social gains from importing a less expensive resource are illustrated. Some of the gains go to the producer and some to the consumer. Restraint of trade in resources eliminates those gains.

An import quota will change the social gain of a good in the following way. Before the quota, the social gain is as follows.

Figure 4.7

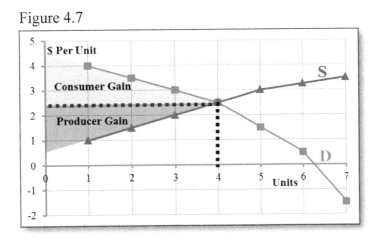

Restricting imports of this good to 2 units (or maybe that is 2 million units) means that the legislated supply curve changes as below—capped at 2 units. With lower supplies for the good, consumers must compete harder to get the product, so the price rises from where it originally was. After import restrictions of Japanese cars in the 1980s, prices went up. People still wanted Japanese cars, since they were better than American cars. But Japanese firms did not have to compete so hard for US business. The green area shows a loss that is not compensated for by anyone—Bastiat calls it a "dead loss." The amazing thing is how much the consumer's gain shrinks and that the producer's gain can increase greatly.

Figure 4.8

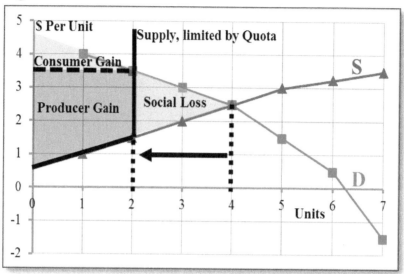

Protectionists may accept imports under some limited conditions, such as:

- The good is impossible to produce domestically in sufficient quantities, eg. diamonds.
- Exporting is good, hence importing is a necessary evil. Hence, if we knew a country would never import our goods, we should never import their goods.
- The exporter has wages and other regulations similar to ours—does not have any great advantages in these areas.
- The imported good will not greatly harm any domestic industry.

So, they would say, if these conditions are not met, we should not import. Thus, the worst foreign source to import from would:

- Produce a good that we produce domestically.
- Never import from us.
- Have zero wages—in fact, sell at a zero price.
- Clearly harm a domestic industry.

Bastiat formulates a response to protectionists in his *Petition of the Candlemakers*. As you listen, note the arguments in which the petitioner reasons that the complex organism of the economy will be improved by a ridiculous suggestion. These sophisms are the same reasons that protectionists offer today.

http://www.youtube.com/watch?v=T52w6dFM3T4 [essential]

This chapter demonstrates how society gains from voluntary trade. It is the means by which the economy grows. For these reasons, the average person today is able to enjoy wonders that only queens and kings of the past could enjoy, such as safe travel, instant communications, variety in music and food, and easy access to information. While many would credit technology with these marvels, remember that no human being can make an iPhone—it takes a worldwide trade network, linked by prices, costs, profits and losses. So technology, alone, gives us nothing without the spontaneous order of an interconnected worldwide market.

Through these processes of value creation—production, in the previous chapter, and trade, in this chapter—we solve **the economic problem** of allocating society's scarce resources to their best uses.

Appendix

Bastiat's discussion of the French hat, which he calls, "an article of millinery," is covered in another essay, but is not well explained in this essay. He was dying from tuberculosis at the time he wrote *What is Seen and What is Not Seen*, so he can be forgiven for the omission. Here is the relevant paragraph from the essay.

> 1.140 James Goodfellow has fifteen francs, the fruit of his labors. (We are back at the time when he is still free.) What does he do with his fifteen francs? He buys an article of millinery for ten francs, and it is with this article of millinery that he pays (or his middleman pays for him) for the hundred kilograms of Belgian iron. He still has five francs left. He does not throw them into the river, but (and this is *what is not seen*) he gives them to some manufacturer or other in exchange for some satisfaction—for example, to a publisher for a copy of the *Discourse on Universal History by Bossuet*.
>
> *Bastiat*

Here is what he means about the hat. James Goodfellow wants to buy iron from Belgium for ten French francs. For this, he needs Belgium's currency. How does he get it?

French hats are popular in Belgium, so James buys a hat from a French hat maker (a milliner) for ten francs and sends the hat to his middleman, who sells the hat it in Belgium for Belgium's currency. With Belgium's currency, the middleman buys the iron James needs from a mine in Belgium and ships the iron to James.

With this part of the example Bastiat points out that James Goodfellow has spent ten francs on a French hat. Also, by buying Belgian iron that is five francs cheaper than Mr. Protectionist's iron, James earns five francs more in profit, which he spends on a book from a French publisher.

So Bastiat demonstrates that even though French iron makers will earn less due to imports, someone in France will earn more, making up that difference. Reckoned from Goodfellow's point of view, with protection he has iron, but with trade he has iron and a book. Reckoned in terms of French commerce, with protection, an iron maker receives fifteen franks, but with trade, a milliner receives ten francs and a publisher receives five.

5

Socialism and Capitalism

SOCIALISM

If we **socialize** an individual's cost or value, we spread it to society, at large. For instance, if the state decides that others should pay for a person's education, the state is in favor of socializing the cost of education. If the state decides that others should receive the benefits of someone's labor, beyond what they are paid for it, the state is in favor of socializing the individual's income.

The market reflects individuals' values of goods and services by people paying private costs to receive things they privately value. When others advocate restricting an individual's freedom to make market decisions, they must assert that they understand the costs and benefits better than the individual who is paying the costs and receiving the benefits that come with his/her decisions. An advocate of *socialism asserts that the individual should act to promote the good of society, not to promote the individual's wellbeing.*

Karl Marx, who is often pointed to as the founder of socialism, said it this way. Production should come "from each, according to his ability, to each, according to his need."

As discussed in Chapter 2, the only alternative to individual economic freedom, which is exercised in markets, is **authoritarian choice**, whether the state's decisions are made by a dictator, the peoples' elected representatives, or by popular vote.

Old and New Rationales for Socialism

An original rationale for socialism was that firms have more power than individuals, so they exploit workers. Socialists countered the obvious argument that exploited workers may quit and work for competitors by asserting that society has rigid classes and that firms are not really in competition with one another for the best workers—they said that Chic-fil-A, Zaxby's, Taco Bell, and McDonalds are, in reality, on the same team.

Another original rationale for socialism was fairness. Socialists, viewing class structures as rigid, said that members of the working class are forever disadvantaged by birth and cannot rise above their station. Given that individuals have no control over which class they are born into, the class system is unfair, so society must be controlled to eliminate the class system.

Marx predicted that as technology advanced that machines would replace workers, which would leave the masses unemployed, able to choose only between starvation and overthrow of the system. However, the predictions of the socialists did not come to pass. By the 1950s, socialists were giving up on their original ways of selling socialism, since there was no reserve army of the unemployed in non-socialist countries and many perceived that people could materially advance beyond their parents' material wellbeing. So socialists devised new rationales. However the exploitation rationale weakly survives, and the fairness rationale—though without the rigid class ideas—is often used to justify socializing costs and benefits.

A modern rationale for socialism is that we must socialize individual decisions by state force in order to counter nature's socializing effects. Some costs naturally spill over to others. These are called **external costs**. Some value also spills over to others. External costs and external benefits are called **externalities**. For instance, a polluting firm imposes costs on others and does not pay those costs. Efficient decision making in society requires that firms pay the costs of their actions, as shown in Chapter 1. With perfect regulation, the state can determine the amount of the costs borne by each individual and force the firm to pay those costs, so production decisions will be efficient, even with pollution. The polluter would, justifiably, reduce production/jobs if the costs can be rightfully assessed. Another externality is created by national defense. If Walmart built a missile defense system, anyone who did not pay would still be able to enjoy the benefits. Because of this, Walmart does not provide national defense, so, since the benefits are naturally socialized, the state socializes the cost, by forcing individuals to pay.

In evaluating the externalities rationale, we must remember Chapter 2 because *efficient assessment of external costs and benefits must be done by those who have knowledge of all facets of the economy and nothing to gain from the regulatory process.* That does not describe any regulator, anywhere. As Chapter 2 made plain, state decision makers protect their own self-interest and are not all-knowing. And, given the quote from Hayek about what kind of people become politicians or regulators in, "Why the Worst Get on Top," we cannot depend on the regulatory process to improve the disadvantages that nature's externalities give us.

Thinking Exercise 5.1 The Chili's Menu

- A snack at Chili's with drink, tax, and tip costs about $10. A normal meal costs about $15. A large meal with appetizers, dessert and margaritas costs about $40.
- In a group of 50 people who were going to eat at Chili's and split the bill evenly, why might someone rather go hungry, rather than order?
- In the group of 50, how much would it cost one individual to buy an appetizer for $5?
- If one person orders an item, but everyone must split the cost of the item evenly, how do we classify the cost that the person imposes on others?
- The organizers of an event held at Chili's noted that some were not eating, which they consider to be bad. At the next event, they construct the following basic Chili's meal and require everyone to pay the cost of $25.67, for which they receive this exact meal;

Table 5.1

Chips & Salsa Appetizer	$3.79
Dr. Pepper	$2.39
Classic Bacon Burger	$8.89
Cheesecake	$5.79
Total costs, including tax & tip	**$25.67**

- What rationale of socialism does this fulfill?
- What issues will likely arise among the attendees?

Maintaining the Socialist Order

In markets, people make decisions by balancing their own values and costs. Since individuals cannot know others' values and costs, making decisions for someone else is inefficient, as discussed in Chapter 2's section on knowledge in society. *Authoritarian decision makers choose for others, based on their own assessments of values and costs.* The central planner must decide if there will be iPhones, hybrid cars, hand-held GPS devices, and the like. Then the central planner must assign all the tasks and acquire the resources necessary for production, based on Marx's principle, "from each, according to his ability." Then the central planner distributes the goods and services, based on Marx's other principle, "to each, according to his need."

If individuals do not agree with the state's assessments of their abilities or with the distribution of goods—for instance, the state must choose who will be an English teacher, an accountant, a heart surgeon, and a carpenter—the state can respond in two ways:

1. Allow individual choice—but this choice will not be based on what the state sees as serving societal wellbeing, so it will not maintain the socialist order.

2. Use force and the threat of force to maintain the socialist order.

Note that it does not matter whether the state's decisions are made by a dictator, elected representatives, or by majority rule, force is necessary when individuals do not agree with the socialist order.

US Socialism

The conception of socialism that this text employs—*the individual should act to promote the good of society, not the individual's wellbeing*—does not differentiate between the various schools of socialist thought. In any form of socialism falling under this definition, the state must take some property rights. Generally if the state takes all property rights, we say that pure communism exists. A system under which the state does not take title to property, but orders the use of that property and the individual in any way it wishes, is a form of **fascism**. It does not matter whether, in reality, the individual is truly serving society or is serving the individuals who run the state—after all, given that no individuals escape serving their own self-interest, all socialist orders serve the individuals who run the state.

US socialism is generally fascistic in nature. The title to your home will likely not be taken by the state, but the design of your home, the design of every appliance in your home, the design of your automobile, and perhaps even your access to your profession are restricted by the state for the good of society.

However, in two areas, outright takings of property are on the rise:

* **Eminent domain**, where property is taken for state public use, such as roads, and parks, but the owner is compensated. Recently "state use" takings of eminent domain include taking property, such as homes, because the state would rather sell the property to business interests.
* **Civil forfeiture**, where a person is suspected of a crime and that person's property is seized because it is automatically suspected as having contributed to the crime. For instance, if a person is found to possess illegal drugs while riding in an automobile, the auto—even if the suspect is not the driver—may be assumed to be used for illegal purposes and may be seized and sold by the state. In addition, the person's home may be confiscated by the state. Typically, the police force that seized the property receives the money or property from the forfeiture. The accused does not have to be convicted of a crime, or even arrested, for the forfeiture to occur. Once the state possesses the individual's property, the individual must sue to recover, which typically costs multiple thousands of dollars, and, in the case of automobiles, is often not worth it. In addition, civil forfeitures are common when individuals possess large amounts of cash, with law enforcement taking the cash and not charging the accused with a crime.

http://www.cato.org/blog/john-oliver-civil-asset-forfeiture [reference]

The latest socialist rationale, popularized in the US, is that if the state provides any good from which the individual might derive external benefits—for example, roads, schools, and courts—that no property is private and the state is justified in dictating the use of the individual's property and income. This rationale of socialism does not take into account the fact that the state originally confiscated individuals' incomes to build the schools, roads, and courts.

The percentage of total spending done by the state is also a measure of the degree of socialism in a nation. Suppose that the state taxes away 100% of incomes and spends to produce goods and services. The only difference between this state and socialism is semantic. The state may not dictate that an individual who wishes to be an accountant must, instead, be an engineer. But if the state hires all the accountants and engineers, the effect is the same. When government spending, as a percentage of total economic activity, grows, the economy becomes more socialistic. Hence, if the state-directed share of the economy rises by

20%, the state has become 20% more socialistic. Bastiat noted the equivalence between the state taking individuals' incomes and commanding individuals to labor in service to the state.

> Money creates an illusion for us. To ask for co-operation, in the form of money, from all the citizens in a common enterprise is, in reality, to ask of them actual physical co-operation, for each one of them procures for himself by his labor the amount he is taxed . . . . Having the citizens contribute money, and not labor, changes nothing in the general results.
>
> *Bastiat*

Reading Exercise 5.1: Read Bastiat Chapter 8: Machines http://www.econlib.org/library/Bastiat/basEss1.html [essential]

- Bastiat says if machines are bad, thinking is bad. Why?
- Which words does Bastiat use to compare trade to technological innovation?
- Bastiat says that some claim that machines simply eliminate jobs. What is his counterclaim?
- Why is James Goodfellow's former employee not doomed to long term unemployment?
- Who benefits from Goodfellow's invention (1) in the short run and (2) in the long run?
- What good comes from the improvements in printing that Bastiat cites?

CAPITALISM

Since this course emphasizes individual decision making and free markets, much has already been said about economic freedom. The previous discussions about markets implied that private property existed in those markets—and private property is an important part of capitalism. Many capitalist philosophers consider the state's only function to be protection of property and persons. From the Declaration of Independence,

> [A]ll men are created equal, that they are endowed by their Creator with certain unalienable Rights, that among these are Life, Liberty and the pursuit of Happiness.— That to secure these rights, Governments are instituted among Men . . . .   *Jefferson*

When those words were written, the right to "**the pursuit of happiness**" meant the right to hold and use property freely, to choose one's profession, to make contracts, and to travel.

In the capitalist view, society's best interest is promoted by individuals with property rights making voluntary decisions. Individuals who wishes to serve their own interest in a society where property rights are protected, cannot steal, so in order to improve their condition they must engage in value-creating production or trade. As individuals continue these activities, they often hire others to further improve. The following quote is by Adam Smith, repeated from Chapter 3.

> [H]e intends only his own gain, and he is . . . led by an invisible hand to promote an end which was no part of his intention . . . . By pursuing his own interest he frequently promotes that of the society more effectually than when he really intends to promote it. I have never known much good done by those who affected to trade for the public good.
>
> *Smith*

Free markets give individuals incentives to voluntarily serve. Socialism divorces consumption from production and, in that way, takes the incentive to voluntarily serve. This is called the **incentive problem** of socialism.

Markets also help solve socialism's "calculation problem." As discussed in Chapter 2, markets connect private information about resource scarcity, individual preferences, and production technologies, encouraging conservation of scarce resources by making their prices higher. Similarly, markets encourage development of substitute resources for those that are scarce. Though socialists favor regulations which they assert will conserve resources—such as ethanol mandates, CAFE standards, and green energy subsidies—capitalists view these regulations as wasteful, since they are not based on individuals' values of the resources and the products they produce, as reflected in market prices. Capitalists charge that socialists rhetorically assert that they understand the value of resources better than individuals who make daily decisions regarding these resources' uses.

Capitalism, Socialism, Fairness

Don Boudreaux, an economist at George Mason University, published the following fairness fable (reprinted with his permission):

> Suppose that Jones chooses a career as a poet. Jones treasures the time he spends walking in the woods and strolling city streets in leisurely reflection; his reflections lead him to write poetry critical of capitalist materialism. Working as a poet, Jones earns $20,000 annually. Smith chooses a career as an emergency-room physician. She works an average of 60 hours weekly and seldom takes a vacation. Her annual salary is $400,000.
>
> - Is this "distribution" of income unfair? Is Smith responsible for Jones' relatively low salary? Does Smith owe Jones money? If so, how much? And what is the formula you use to determine Smith's debt to Jones?
> - While Dr. Smith earns more money than does poet Jones, poet Jones earns more leisure than does Dr. Smith.
> - Do you believe leisure has value to those who possess it?
> - If so, are you disturbed by the inequality of leisure that separates leisure-rich Jones from leisure-poor Smith?
> - Do you advocate policies to "redistribute" leisure from Jones to Smith—say, by forcing Jones to wash Smith's dinner dishes or to chauffeur Smith to and from work? If not, why not?

http://triblive.com/opinion/donaldboudreaux/5283716-74/jones-smith-income#ixzz31uFO8qgb [reference]

Boudreaux's story illustrates that people who push the limits of their abilities earn more than they could if they do not, in the same way that students who sacrifice, in order to study exhaustively, tend to earn better grades than if they do not. People who play *Call of Duty* and watch *Seinfeld* reruns, instead of trying to fill every spare minute with gainful employment, voluntarily sacrifice money for other satisfactions. Neither way is necessarily right, but both ways are based on people paying the cost of their actions. This does not imply that everyone has equal endowments of talent, beauty, emotional stability, and strength, but capitalist philosophers like Boudreaux point out that we cannot calculate how to compensate for these endowments.

Socialists concentrate on pointing out only the differences in income, without respect to how those differences came to be and propose that the state use force (taxation, backed by armed agents) to correct the differences in income generated in large part by the differences in individuals' natural endowments, including ambition. Thomas Piketty and Emmanuel Saez (P&S) used US tax data to conclude that incomes in the United States have become more and more unequal since the 1980s. They estimate that incomes of top earners grew by nearly 200%, while the average taxpayer's income stagnated, growing by only 3% over the thirty year period. http://elsa.berkeley.edu/~saez/piketty-saezOUP04US.pdf [reference]

While socialists welcome these results, because one of their "fairness rationale," others who approach the problem differently get different results. In particular, Burkhauser, Larrimore, and Simon (BLS) show that P&S's result is only one viewpoint. BLS points out that,

- P&S use individual taxpayer data, since they cannot derive household income from their data. Since the 1980s, households have changed greatly—with more people living together without marriage. Hence, P&S's data might contain an impoverished individual and a wealthy individual, who happen to live in the same household. The female, a heart surgeon, provides the income while the male cares for children and is a freelance writer. In reality, the household is wealthy, but P&S miss these social changes.

- P&S measure before-tax income. Taxes have fallen greatly since the 1980s, so take-home pay has increased, relative to the 1980s.

- If we must count taxes, we should also count transfer payments, such as Social Security and Medicare. This shrinks the income differential, as well.

- Since the 1980s employee fringe benefits have increased greatly, compared to wages, now making up a third of total pay. P&S capture only money income and not fringe benefits.

- Using individual taxpayer data misses synergies of households. Two people living in two different households, who moved in together, whether married or not, cut their expenses by sharing rent payments and other household payments.

- Adjusting for these factors, the P&S 3% increase in income becomes a 37% increase.

To this, Thomas Sowell adds the fact that when we picture "the top earners" and "the poor" we see unchanging groups of individuals, but this is not the case. Sowell's first point is that the poorest, by age, are in their teens and twenties. The richest, by age, are old. As the poor young people age, they gain education and experience and get richer. The top income earners are those who are nearing retirement. Sowell's second point is that each picture of an income group is like a photo, but photos taken at different times have different people in the picture. People sometimes gain income and sometimes lose income, making categories less useful than the news media or some researchers realize. http://www.crisismagazine.com/2011/of-inequality-and-numbers-games [essential]

> [M]ost of the working people who were in the bottom 20 percent of income earners in 1975 were also in the top 40 percent at some point by 1991. Only 5 percent of those in the bottom quintile in 1975 were still there in 1991, while 29 percent of them were now in the top quintile.
>
> *Sowell*

This does not mean that capitalism is perfect. Markets do not solve all fairness problems, but, given the calculation problem and a self-interested state, governments might not do any better. In any case, people do not agree on definitions of fairness. Here is a common capitalist formulation of the topic, given in question form:

- Is it fair that a professional athlete, whom millions, worldwide, enjoy watching, has a much higher income than a teacher of 25 students?
- How scarce are Lebron James-quality athletes, compared to the generic teacher that is held up in this common example?
- If the athlete with rare talents and skills should be rewarded more, then should the CEO of a large corporation be rewarded more, given that only a small number of individuals are able to perform well at that level?
- Should rare talent be rewarded by individuals who wish to purchase that talent, or should a central decision maker decide who should have which rewards?

With regard to the socialists' "fairness" rationale, capitalist philosophers point to the results of the two systems. This is Milton Friedman on how capitalism improves the material condition of the populace, at large. http://www.youtube.com/watch?v=76frHHpoNFs [essential]

In our present system, we socialize the care for the poor using tax revenues. "In total, the United States spends nearly $1 trillion every year to fight poverty. That amounts to $20,610 for every poor person in America, or $61,830 per poor family of three." http://www.cato.org/sites/cato.org/files/pubs/pdf/PA694.pdf [reference]

The massive US state bureaucracy faces such a large calculation problem that decision makers have no idea how so much could be spent, though the poverty rate is 16%, about the same as it was forty years ago when the state spent much less. In the graph below are poverty rates, found by the Census Bureau and economic growth rates from the Bureau of Economic Analysis. The growth rate is lagged by three years to reflect the fact that economic growth may take some time to affect those in poverty. Though we do not see a downward trend in poverty rates, as the state spends more to fight poverty, we can see that the two lines mirror each other. When economic growth falls, poverty eventually rises. When economic growth rises, poverty eventually falls. Thus, an efficient economy that creates value can help poverty. As this chapter and Chapter 2 reveal, though, an intrusive state makes the economy weaker and harms the poor. The extreme version of this is found in Chapter 2's illustration of the two Koreas.

Figure 5.1

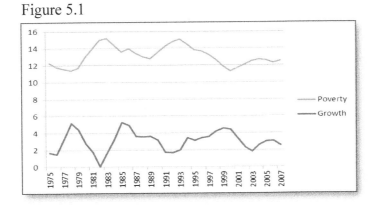

In a free economy, individuals contribute income in order help others and there is competition between nonprofit firms to provide the most and best aid. Though the economy was unhealthy in 2011, individuals gave over $300 billion in cash to charitable causes. In addition to cash, individuals also contributed labor, goods, and services.

Those who say that private giving could not replace government giving should recall *status quo minus* fallacy from Chapter 2. As government expands its attempts to help, voluntary giving declines. Before government provided unemployment insurance, churches and mutual aid societies were active in providing unemployment insurance. Before government schools, there were more private and religious schools. Since private markets for assisting others existed before government took their place, there is every reason to think that they would reemerge if government retreated from "the fairness business," and concentrated on protecting life, liberty and property.

Thinking Exercise 5.2 Fairness in the Classroom

A professor has heard many times that some students do worse in class because of circumstances beyond their control, such as,

- Illness
- Caring for sick relatives
- Family problems that cause worries
- Learning disabilities
- Extra-curricular activities that scholarships depend on
- Jobs that are necessary to continue going to school
- A poor K-12 education due to living in a bad school district

He realizes that many, if not all, these claims are real, and, further, some who have these problems never tell him about them. So he has decided to institute a new grading system to improve fairness.

Just as a social planner has two goals—efficiency (encouraging efficient resource use) and fairness, the professor would like the grading system to be efficient (encouraging learning) and fair.

He comes up with two plans, by which to assign grades on the three tests he will give. He will choose one of the plans listed below:
1. Figure out a fair curve for each of the above problems, inform the students about it, ask the students which of the problems they each have, and apply the curve, student by student.
2. Give each student the entire class' average grade on each test.

Do the following:
- Figure out a fair curve for each of the special student circumstances described above.
- How fair would the results from each of the two plans be?
- How efficient (encouraging learning) would each of the two plans be?
- Can you devise a way of *improving* on the usual method of making assignments and giving each individual the grade they made on their own assignment, with no adjustment for circumstances like those above? By "improving" I mean making more fairness without harming efficiency or more efficiency without harming fairness.

Money and Prices

The following is from Bastiat's essay, *What is Money?* with minor adjustments to modernize the translation:

> Ten persons were gambling. For greater ease, they had adopted the plan of *each* taking ten chips, and against these they *each* placed one hundred francs under a candlestick, so that each chip corresponded to ten francs. After the game the winnings were adjusted, and the players drew from under the candlestick as many francs as would represent the number of chips.
>
> Seeing this, one of them, a great arithmetician perhaps, but an indifferent reasoner, said: "Gentlemen, experience invariably teaches me that, at the end of the game, I find myself a gainer in proportion to the number of my chips. Have you not observed the same with regard to yourselves? Thus, what is true of me must be true of each of you, and what is true of each must be true of all. We should, therefore, all of us gain more, at the end of the game, if we all had more chips. Now, nothing can be easier; we have only to [start the game with twenty chips each]."
>
> This was done; but when the game was finished, and they came to adjust the winnings, it was found that the francs under the candlestick had not been miraculously multiplied, according to the general expectation. [It] had to be divided accordingly, and the only result obtained was this: every one had, it is true, his double number of chips, but every chip, instead of corresponding to ten francs, only represented five.
>
> Thus it was clearly shown that what is true of each is not always true of all.
>
> *Bastiat*

http://mises.org/library/what-money [reference]

Chapter 3 made clear that true material wellbeing does not come from money, but from goods and services, as Adam Smith said, "the wealth of a country consists, not in its gold and silver only, but in its lands, houses, and consumable goods of all different kinds."

Smith told us what money is not. Bastiat said, "it is absolutely necessary to forget money, coins, bank notes, and the other media by which products pass from hand to hand, in order to see only the products themselves, which constitute the real substance . . . . Money makes its appearance only to facilitate the arrangement among several parties." That is, **money** is anything that is generally acceptable in making exchanges, so that people who make pizzas for a living and want to buy gasoline can sell for money and buy with money.

The alternative to money exchange is **barter**—trading without the use of widely accepted means of exchange. Using barter, to buy gas the pizza maker must find a gas station owner who wants lots of pizza. That is, to exchange with barter there must exist a **double coincidence of wants**.

People first traded by bartering goods and services, but soon noticed that some goods were easier to trade for than others. These goods evolved into money. Money developed because it was superior to barter, since double coincidence of wants is a terrible inconvenience. Smith lists the following commodities that evolved into money:

- Labor (the original common medium of exchange)
- Cattle (early societies)
- Salt (early societies, including Rome)
- Cowry shells (India)
- Cod (Newfoundland)
- Tobacco (early Virginia)
- Sugar (West Indies)
- Iron (Sparta)
- Copper (Rome)
- Gold and silver (many societies throughout history)

One of the strangest forms of money ever used are the rai stones on the Pacific island of Yap. http://en.wikipedia.org/wiki/Rai_stones [reference] In the past, cigarettes were used as money in US prisons, but now other goods, notably mackerel, are used. http://online.wsj.com/article/SB122290720439096481.html [reference]

A good is more likely to evolve into money if it fulfills the following **functions of money**:

1. Medium of exchange—it is generally acceptable and convenient for exchange.

2. Unit of account—each unit of it is "worth" the same amount.

3. Store of value—it retains value over time.

Money might have other uses, such as the items in Smith's list, in which case it is called **commodity money**. Money might not have any other use, in which case it is called **fiat money**.

Thinking Exercise 6.1: Good Money

Which of the functions of money would the following not fulfill?
- Labor
- Cattle
- Salt
- Cowry shells
- Cod
- Rai stones
- Vacuum sealed packs of mackerel

True or False, Explain: If a commodity becomes money, then no one will use it as a commodity.

True or False, Explain: For a commodity to function well as money, it must be impossible for a person to manufacture or discover more of it on their own.

A CURRENT DEFINITION OF MONEY: M1

In the US, dollars are money—either in the form of green tinted sheets made from cotton or in the form of bits and bytes in an account. The wellspring of all US dollars is the Federal Reserve System and the banking system. There are a few different measurements of our money supply, which differ by **liquidity**—the ease with which an asset can be converted to spendable form. The most referenced measurement is **M1** (pronounced, "M One"), which most of us think of as money. M1 is the sum of;

- Paper currency held outside banks,
- Checking account balances,
- Travelers' Checks (nearly obsolete http://en.wikipedia.org/wiki/Traveler%27s_cheque). [reference]

***As of this writing, M1 is about $2.9 trillion. You can check for the latest numbers and look at the historical size of M1 here: http://research.stlouisfed.org/fred2/series/M1/ [essential]

***By way of comparison, the total income received in our economy is now about $17.3 trillion. http://www.bea.gov/newsreleases/national/gdp/gdpnewsrelease.htm [reference]

THE FED AND THE MONEY CREATION PROCESS

Structure and Tools of The Fed

The US Federal Reserve, which now creates every US dollar that exists in the world, was established in 1913 to stabilize the banking system through being a lender of last resort to troubled banks. Previous banking crises were handled by large banks, such as J. P. Morgan, but the state wanted to take control of that process, thinking they could prevent future crises. Within fifteen years, Fed errors caused a huge deflation that is now credited by Friedman, Hayek, Mises, and many other economists as the root cause of the Great Depression.

The Fed does not depend on congress for a budget—it finances itself. It was intended to be a government-business partnership with shared governance. The business interests of various regions of the US were to be represented by the twelve district banks as seen at http://www.federalreserve.gov/otherfrb.htm [reference]. However, the district banks today have a minor voice in the Fed. Government interests are represented by the board of governors which includes:

- Seven governors, appointed by the President with the advice and consent of the Senate, who serve fourteen year terms.
- A chairman, who is appointed by the US President every four years, who must also face confirmation by the US Senate.

Through the use of **monetary policy**, the Fed uses the money supply to attempt to affect the economy. The way that the money supply affects the economy will be fully developed in this chapter and the next. For now, the focus is on the money creation tools and process, not on the money supply's effect on the economy.

The **Federal Open Market Committee** conducts monetary policy. It is composed of:
- The Board of Governors (which has seven members)
- The President of the New York Federal Reserve Bank
- The Presidents of the other eleven district banks, four of whom vote at each meeting on a rotating basis

Although the majority rules, the Fed chairman's recommendations are nearly always adopted unanimously because voting against the chairman is looked down upon.

The **three tools of monetary policy** are:

- **Open Market Operations**—buying and selling US government bonds from individuals and businesses who previously bought them from the US government. When the Fed buys bonds, bonds flow into the Fed and money flows into the economy, increasing the money supply, and vice versa,
- **The Required Reserve Ratio**—the Fed sets the required reserve ratio, which is the percentage of deposits that banks cannot lend out, but must hold as reserves,
  - **A bank's reserves** consist of its vault cash plus the bank's account with the Fed,
  - **Excess reserves** are reserves that banks hold in excess of those the Fed requires,
  - At any point in time, a bank can lend out its excess reserves,
  - The current required reserve ratio is 10%,
  - With a lower required reserve ratio, banks can lend more, and vice versa,
  - This creates new money—remember, money inside bank vaults or at the Fed *is not* part of the money supply, while money in household and business accounts *is* part of the money supply,
- **The Discount Rate**—the Fed was created to be a lender of last resort. That is, they are the final stop that a bank makes for an emergency loan before it fails. When a bank borrows from the Fed, it pays an interest rate called **the discount rate** which the Fed sets by command.

When the Fed lends, a clerk inside the Fed taps a few keys on a keyboard and the troubled bank then has more millions in its account with the Fed, which it can then use to stay afloat by paying creditors. This represents new money being created.

In creating money, *the Fed's target is the Federal Funds Rate,* which is *a free market rate* at which banks lend to other banks. If the Fed puts money into the banking system, it is easier to borrow, so the Federal Funds Rate falls. If the press reports, "The Fed met today and lowered interest rates by a point," they mean, "The Federal Open Market Committee met today and decided to increase the money supply until the free market Federal Funds Rate falls by a point."

The Fed prefers to use open market operations, rather than the other two tools. The required reserve ratio can cause dangerous swings in bank lending. If banks were only borrowing to profit themselves, a lower discount rate would generally attract more banks to borrow, increasing the money supply. But borrowing from the Fed shows weakness to the public and to the bank's regulators, and banks run on maintaining public confidence. However, in extreme situations, the Fed encourages borrowing. This ambivalence makes the discount rate a weak tool.

Since 2008, the number of tools in the Fed's kit is unknown, since they adopted unforeseen and unheard of policies, including auctioning off funds, buying commercial paper, buying mortgage backed securities, opening the discount window to investment banks, such as Goldman-Sachs, and paying interest on banks' reserves held at the Fed. Currently, officials at the Fed will not admit to any bounds on their authority to buy and sell in the marketplace.

The Money Creation Process

If the Fed wishes to increase the money supply they use one of the three tools. Suppose they decide to buy a $1,000 US bond from a consumer.

- The consumer gives up a bond and $1,000 goes into the consumer's bank account. Money in consumers' bank accounts is part of the money supply, so this is $1,000 in new money.

- The consumer's bank now has more deposits, so it can lend more. It must keep some of the deposit as reserves—$100 if the required reserve ratio is 10%. Suppose the bank lends its new excess reserves—$900—to a consumer who buys a computer from Best Buy.
- Now Best Buy's bank has $900 in its account. Suppose it lends its excess reserves of $810 (keeping the $90 in required reserves) to someone who buys furniture.
- The furniture company's bank account now has $810, which is also money.
- And so on.
- Our original consumer can spend the $1,000 in the bank account, and Best Buy can spend the $900 and the furniture company can spend the $810, and so on.
- The original Fed injection of money has multiplied throughout the banking system.
- The formula for finding the eventual increase in the money supply is $1,000 divided by the required reserve ratio = $1,000/.1 = $10,000.
- The general formula for the simple money multiplier is 1/(required reserve ratio).
- For any change in excess reserves, such as the Fed's injection of $1,000, the expansion of the money supply, throughout the banking system, is the size of the injection multiplied by the money multiplier.

Money expands through the banking system through the process of lending, relending, and more relending. This is how the money that is now in our accounts was created in the first place.

PRICES AND INFLATION DEFINITION

One way that money simplifies exchange in the economy is by giving a common unit of account. A particular combo meal has a price of $7.49, whereas if chickens were money, the price of the combo meal would depend on the value of the chicken(s) offered in exchange, and different chickens do not have the same value.

All dollars have the same value. The **value of the dollar in the domestic economy** depends on how many and which goods and services it will buy. We usually turn the problem around—how many dollars does it take to buy a unit of goods and services. Then we must specify what we mean by "a unit of goods and services," by choosing a typical market basket of goods and services—picture a month's worth of goods and services that a typical consumer buys.

In deriving the **Consumer Price Index** (CPI), each month the Bureau of Labor Statistics (BLS) measures prices of 200 goods that a typical consumer buys, from a fancy parakeet, to a rental payment on a home, to a fifteen-minute visit with a family doctor. The measurement is a weighted average of the prices—weighted by the amounts of the goods that consumers purchase.

The CPI is the most cited price measure, but there are others, such as the Federal Reserve's measure, the **PCE price index** (personal consumption expenditures index), which excludes food and fuel, which make up 20% of household purchases.

Calculating and Using Price Indices

Thinking Exercise 6.2: Finding a CPI

Here are a few important items that consumers purchase each month, their prices last December, and their prices next December.

- Find the total spent last December.
- Find the total spent next December.
- Fill in the blanks: The stuff that costs _____ last December, costs _____ next Dec.
- Using your fill in the blank answer above, answer this question: If $1.00 bought $1.00 worth of stuff last December, how much would it cost to buy that same stuff next December?
- By what percentage have prices increased?

Table 6.1

Item	Monthly Purchases	Price Last December	Price Next December	Spent Last September	Spent Next December
Gallon of Gas	80	$3.50	$6.00		
14" 1 Topping Pizza	5	$10.00	$30.00		
Rent	1	$300.00	$630.00		
Total Spent					

Price indices, such as the CPI measure prices by comparing the cost of a market basket at a period of time (a focal period) to the cost of the same market basket in some reference year (base year). For instance, one might say that prices now (the focal period) are twice what they were in 1983 (the base period). The price index is found like this.

PI = (cost of market basket in focal period) / (cost of market basket in base period) x 100

Your answer to the next-to-last question in Thinking Exercise 6.2 is a price index number—if you multiply it by 100.

This is the most straightforward *interpretation of a price index*. It answers this question:

So if the price index is 300, then if $100 bought $100 worth of stuff in the base period, today it would cost $300 to buy the same stuff.

Thinking Exercise 6.3: Finding another CPI

Here are a few important items that consumers purchase each month, their prices last May, and their prices May-before-last.

- Find the total spent May-before-last.
- Find the total spent last May.
- Fill in the blanks: The stuff that costs _____ May-before-last, costs _____ last May.
- Using your fill in the blank answer above, answer: if $1 bought $1 worth of stuff May-before-last, how much would it cost to buy that same stuff last May?
- Find the CPI.
- By what percentage have prices increased?

Table 6.2

Item	Monthly Purchases	Price May Before Last	Price Last May	Spent May Before Last	Spent Last May
Gallon of Gas	80	$3.50	$3.95		
14" 1 Topping Pizza	5	$10.00	$9.00		
Rent	1	$300.00	$320.00		
Total Spent					

Thinking Exercise 6.2 gives a reference point for thinking about price indices. Thinking Exercise 6.3 lets you use the same technique to make sure you have a general understanding of price indices.

Here is the CPI: http://data.bls.gov/cgi-bin/surveymost?bls [essential]. Under the "Price Indexes" heading, choose the top selection and click "Retrieve Data" at the bottom of the page. Then, beside "Change Output Options," change the "From" year to 1980 and choose "Go," to the right.

Note that above the table, it says the base period is 1982-1984. The numbers in those years are about 100. This is because in the price index formula, if the base period is also the period of focus, the calculation yields 100. In Thinking Exercise 6.3, you answered this question:

- If $100 bought $100 worth of stuff May-before-last, how much would it cost to buy that same stuff last May?

Consider a slightly different question

- If $100 bought $100 worth of stuff *May-before-last*, how much would it cost to buy that same stuff *May-before-last*?

Since the answer to the second question will always be $100, the price index in the base period is always 100.

Measuring Inflation

Thinking Exercise 6.4: Using CPI Data

- What is the CPI for November, 2012?
- Fill in the blanks using this numbers and concepts in this table. $1 bought $1 worth of stuff in the year _____. But in November, 2012 _____.
- By what percentage did prices increase from the base period to January 1990?
- By what percentage did prices increase from the base period to January 2000?
- By what percentage did prices increase from the base period to November 2012?
- By approximately what percentage did prices increase from January 1988 to November 2012?
- By what percentage did prices increase from November 2011 to November 2012?

Inflation is the percentage change in the price index, usually over a year's time. To find the inflation from year 1 to year 2, use

$$\text{Inflation}_{Y1toY2} = (CPI_{Y2} / CPI_{Y1}) - 1$$

Adjusting Data for Price Changes

Thinking Exercise 6.5: How Well Off When?

Answer the following questions by accounting for price changes over the time period. Use the CPI data.

- Mom made $50,000 per year in January of 2000. How much would she have to make in November of 2012 to be just as well off?
- Dad made $30,000 per year in January of 2000 and made $40,000 in November of 2012. When was Dad better off?
- Uncle Fester made $20,000 per year in November of 2012. If he were just as well of in January of 2000, then he must have been making _____?

There are many ways to work the problems in Thinking Exercise 6.5, which focus on how well off people are in different years, accounting for price changes. One way is to start with some intuition and proceed to a formula. Here is the intuition. If prices had doubled from January 2000 to November 2012, then Mom would need to make twice as much to be just as well off—$100,000. If prices had doubled, then $1 worth of stuff in January 2000 would cost $2 in November 2012—such as, if the CPI were 168.8 in January 2000 and 337.6 in November 2012. We could use this formula to find the answer this way.

$$\text{Equivalent Income}_{\text{New}} = \text{CPI}_{\text{New}}/\text{CPI}_{\text{Old}} \text{ x Income}_{\text{Old}}$$

$$\text{Equivalent Income}_{\text{New}} = 337.6/168.8 \text{ x } \$50,000$$

$$\text{Equivalent Income}_{\text{New}} = 2 \text{ x } \$50,000$$

The ratio of the CPIs tells you this. If $1 bought $1 worth of stuff in 2000, then to buy the same stuff today, you would need $2. So for each of the old 50,000 $1 dollar bills, you would need $2 in November 2012. So you would need $100,000 in November 2012.

This formula works, in general.

- If Auntie Em earned $20,000 in January 1980, what is the equivalent income, adjusting for price changes in November 2012?
- First we look up the two CPIs at the BLS web site.
- CPI_{New} = 230.221. CPI_{Old} = 77.8
- $\text{Equivalent Income}_{\text{New}} = \text{CPI}_{\text{New}}/\text{CPI}_{\text{Old}} \text{ x Income}_{\text{Old}}$
- $\text{Equivalent Income}_{\text{New}}$ = 230.221/77.8 x $20,000
- $\text{Equivalent Income}_{\text{New}}$ = 2.96 x $20,000
- The ratio of the CPIs tells you this. If $1 bought $1 worth of stuff in 1980, in November 2012 it would take $2.96 to buy the same stuff. So for each of the old 20,000 one dollar bills, Em would need $2.96. So she would need
- $\text{Equivalent Income}_{\text{New}}$ = $2.96 x 20,000 = $59,182.78
- Also note that 2.96 - 1 = 1.96, which tells us that the total amount of inflation from January 1980 to November 2012 is 196%. That is, prices have nearly tripled, so that is 200% inflation. (Note: some people think that if prices triple, then the amount of inflation should be 300%. But remember, if there has been 100% inflation, prices doubled.)

For Uncle Fester's problem in Thinking Exercise 6.5, you can take the formula and switch the "New" and "Old" notations.

For Dad's problem in Thinking Exercise 6.5, you can either find the equivalent income in November 2012, then compare to the actual income. Or you can use a formula for "Real Income" to find the answer. **Nominal income** is the number on the paycheck. **Real income** expresses nominal income in terms of base period prices. That is, a series of real income numbers focuses on how much stuff you can buy, eliminating the effects of price changes. If we just apply the New/Old formula, changing the labels we get the following:

Uncle Leo earned $60,000 in January 2000 and $75,000 in January 2008. When was Uncle Leo better off? To get the answer we put both incomes in terms of base year prices.

Start with the old formula: Equivalent Income$_{New}$ = CPI$_{New}$/CPI$_{Old}$ x Income$_{Old}$

Switching for the labels Base and Focus, we get:

Real Income in Focus Year = Equivalent Income$_{Base}$ = CPI$_{Base}$/CPI$_{Focus}$ x Income$_{Focus}$

Real Income in 2000 = 100/168.8 x $60,000 = $60,000 / 1.688 = $35,545.02

Real Income in 2008 = 100/211.080 x $75,000 = $75,000 / 2.11080 = $35,531.55

So Uncle Leo was slightly better off in 2000.

Both of those numbers we derived were putting income into base year (1982-1984) dollars.

Look back at what happens in calculating a real income. We just take the income we are focused on then divide by the price index, expressed not in 100s, but in 1s. So if we want to find a real income for a focal income of $80,000 in a year where the CPI is 200, then we just divide the $80,000 by 2. That is, if prices doubled since the base year, it would have taken only half the income in the base year to be just as well off.

Where real income comes in exceptionally handy is when one looks at how much someone made in a number of years. For instance, here is Aunt Bea's nominal income for the 2000s.

Table 6.3

Year	Nominal Income	CPI (Annual)	Real Income
2000	$100,000	172.2	$58,072
2001	$103,000	177.1	$58,159
2002	$106.090	179.9	$58,972
2003	$109,272	184.0	$59,387
2004	$112,551	188.9	$59,582
2005	$115,927	195.3	$59,359
2006	$119,405	201.6	$59,229
2007	$122,987	207.342	$59,316
2008	$126,677	215.303	$58,836
2009	$130,477	214.537	$60,818
2010	$145,000	218.056	$61,631

Using the annual CPIs, we take each year's income back to the base year, so we can compare how much stuff she could buy in the different years if prices had not changed. We see that at first she had a small gain: $58,072 up to $58,159. After three more years her real income falls slightly, though her paycheck keeps rising. This means that inflation is going up faster than her paycheck. Her real income—her ability to purchase stuff—is mostly down until 2009, when she has a respectable gain, then again in 2010. Though she got raises in nominal income every year, her real income mostly fell—she couldn't buy as much stuff—until the last two years when she more than made up the difference.

The following graphic adjusts game console prices at launch for inflation—putting them all in 2012 dollars. That is, these are the real prices, using 2012 as a base year. Companies adjust their prices along with inflation to build a marketing strategy. Though companies must base their prices on costs and value, they can decide to build products with expensive features or not. These strategies determine who their customers are, how many units they will sell, and at what prices. That is, these strategies help determine the company's profitability.

Figure 6.1

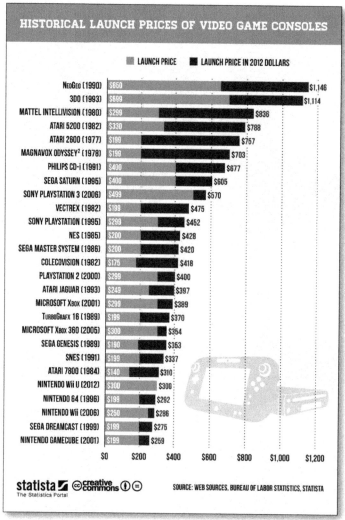

These kinds of numbers are important for a business's earnings, the average worker's wages, a school board's budget, or a charitable foundation's endowment. It is important for a person to know whether they are beating inflation or whether inflation is beating them.

Causes and Effects of Inflation

WHERE INFLATION COMES FROM

The Equation of Exchange

Could an increase in the price of gasoline give rise to inflation? The argument in favor is that gasoline is used in producing and transporting every good, so as all those costs rose, all prices must rise. However, it turns out that this only looks at half of the story.

If the price of gasoline rises, consumers react by purchasing less gasoline, but they almost surely spend more, in total, on gasoline. If consumers spend more on gasoline, they must spend less on other goods—that is, the demands for other goods fall. But this causes the prices of other goods to fall, so we cannot get a general inflation from an increase in the price of gasoline. We only get relative price changes.

The only way consumers can spend more on <u>all</u> goods is if there are more dollars available to spend—the money supply must increase. The **equation of exchange** shows the relationship between prices and the money supply.

MV = PQ, where

- M is the money supply
- P is the price level
- Q is the amount of output produced by the economy

Here are what the equation means. Since P is the price of the output and Q is the amount of the output, PQ is the amount spent on the output at the current price level—the total amount of spending in the economy. ***This amount is currently more than $15 trillion (really $17.3T). Earlier, we saw that M1 is about $2.5T (it is $2.9T). If we substitute for what we know,

$2.5 trillion x V = $15 trillion

With some algebra, we find V = 6. But we have not yet defined V. However, V answers this question. "How can 2.5 trillion dollars purchase the 15 trillion dollars' worth of output that was produced during the year?"

The way that this can happen is by the money supply "turning over." That is, any dollars in our pockets or in our bank account came from somewhere, and they will go to somewhere, and they will go on from there. So the money supply turns over to purchase output. The average number of times that $1 turns over is called V—velocity. (Note, this is not the same as the money creation process that we discussed earlier, which involved banks lending and relending.)

So MV = PQ just means that the output in the economy is bought by the money supply, which is spent and re-spent at a rate of V. This is *the interpretation of the equation of exchange.*

This observation is so obvious that no economist disagrees with it. It was formulated by John Stuart Mill in the late 1800s and was put into equation form by Irving Fisher in the early 1900s.

The Simple Quantity Theory

The simple quantity theory, developed by Irving Fisher and Ludwig von Mises in the early 1900s, begins with the equation of exchange and adds two observations:

- Over a short time period, resources are limited, so output is limited.
- The speed at which money moves through the economy is limited.

In fact, the simple quantity theory assumes that in the short run, output and velocity are constant—just numbers that cannot change. Substituting into the equation of exchange, and assuming that we are producing 7.5 trillion units of output,

$$\$2.5 \text{ trillion} \times 6 = \$2 \times 7.5 \text{ trillion}$$

That is, $2.5 trillion turns over 6 times per year to purchase $15 trillion worth of output, and that output consists of 7.5 trillion units, each at a price of $2. Since V and Q are assumed constant, we keep them as numbers, but let M and P vary.

$$M \times 6 = P \times 7.5 \text{ trillion}$$

Suppose the Federal Reserve doubles the money supply to $5 trillion through a bond purchase and the banking system's multi-stage creation of money, through lending and relending, as discussed in chapter 6. Substituting in for M, then solving for P,

$$\$5 \text{ trillion} \times 6 = P \times 7.5 \text{ trillion}$$
$$\$30 \text{ trillion} = P \times 7.5 \text{ trillion}$$
Hence, P increases to $4

So when the money supply doubles, the price level doubles. Similarly, if the money supply halved, the price level would half and if the money supply rose by 10% the price level would rise by 10%. That is, *the result of the simple quantity theory is that the price level and the money supply are proportionally related.*

This is the basic answer to the question posed by this section—"Where does inflation come from?" In our economy, inflation comes from the Fed and the banking system increasing the money supply. Most countries that increase the money supply quickly are trying to speed up the economy, increasing output (Q), in order to reduce unemployment. We assumed Q was constant over the short run. What follows is a theory that allows for more variation in Q.

Monetarism

Milton Friedman founded the monetarist school of economics. His book, *A Monetary History of the United States*, coauthored with Anna Schwartz, published in 1963, changed the economics profession. Monetarism begins with the equation of exchange, then softens the assumptions of the simple quantity theory.

- While the simple quantity theory assumed that velocity is fixed, Friedman and Schwartz showed, using 100 years of data, that velocity, while not fixed, does not change much. Velocity is a stable function of a few variables, so velocity is predictable and stable.

- While the simple quantity theory assumed that output is fixed in the short run, monetarism assumes that output is not fixed—but that the economy has a potential that it tends to move toward. Here is why the potential exists: monetarism assumes that the labor market is in equilibrium in the long run, with the amount of labor supplied equal to the amount of labor demanded. Chapter 3 discusses fully employed resources—the production possibilities frontier shows our potential output if we have fully employed resources. So if the labor market is in equilibrium, our output is at its potential. Hence, Friedman says free markets work, giving equilibria and moving us to the PPF in the long run.

With these two additions to the simple quantity theory, we consider the equation of exchange: $MV = PQ$, stating the assumptions of monetarism. On the left hand side, velocity can be considered stable. On the right hand side, output can vary somewhat in the short run, but in the long run tends toward its potential, which occurs where the labor market is in equilibrium.

Friedman illustrates his ideas with "the helicopter drop of dollars" story, reprinted in *Money Mischief*. It goes like this, with the economy-wide interpretation in italics.

A helicopter flies over a city and drops one million $100 bills. First people scoop up money—some ending up with $50,000, some ending up with $250,000, and others ending up with more. That night, a person with a quarter of a million dollars is likely to leave the Hot Pockets in the freezer and drive to the steak house.

(The Federal Reserve has increased the money supply to stimulate the economy, hoping to reduce unemployment.)

There is a line at the steak house because of the new money. The owner of the steak house realizes that she will run out of steaks before the night is through. Further, the owner realizes that if the price of a steak were $100, instead of $20, that she would still run out of steak. So does every other place in town. So everyone raises their prices, and sends employees to the grocery store to buy steak. So in the short run, prices rise and quantities rise and the steakhouse owner starts to look for more employees to produce even more steak to grab more of the helicopter dollars.

(According to the equation of exchange, the increase in the money supply makes prices rise. Monetarism says there may be some gains in output—Q—in the short run. And employment rises in the short run.)

But there are problems for the steakhouse manager. Many of <u>her employees</u> scooped up a few dozen thousand dollars and are more interested in throwing parties than in being given a hard time by customers. And with the line so long, the employer needs even more employees than usual, so she calls in people from all shifts, has to pay overtime, and has to pay huge wages to get people to be interested in working. Wages also rise as the seafood restaurant offers to pay the steak house employees more money, so that the seafood restaurant can scoop up more helicopter dollars. Also, with everybody in town buying more stuff, the price of raw steak, raw potatoes and prices of the other resources rise.

(The increase in demand for labor and for other resources pushes resource prices up, hence the cost of producing output rises.)

By the end of the week, with steakhouse prices higher, but with the prices of all the resources higher, the line at the steakhouse is back to normal, and employment falls to what it was before the helicopter drop.

(In the long run, with higher prices, the <u>real</u> wage, the <u>real</u> price of a steak dinner, and all other <u>real</u> prices are the same as before. In the long run, the helicopter drop only causes inflation.)

So when the Federal Reserve creates money, monetarists say they might boost growth and employment in the short run, but in the long run the Fed only causes inflation. With regard to continuing inflation, Friedman and the monetarists say, "Inflation is, always and everywhere, a monetary phenomenon." If we see a country with an inflation problem, we always see a central bank that is creating lots of money.

EFFECTS OF INFLATION ON THE ECONOMY

The pizza place example is used for much of the chapter. If a test question asks about "the pizza place example," it will refer to the formulation below, not on realistic refinements that follow.

The Pizza Place Example

You own a pizza place. You are able to charge $10 for a pizza that costs a total of $8 to produce. Then all prices in the economy double. Should you . . .

    a.   produce more
    b.   produce less
    c.   produce the same amount
    d.   not be able to decide without more information

This example will be useful for the rest of the course. All prices double—that includes the price of:

- Your pizza,
- The resources that make the pizza—your costs, and
- Everything you buy as a consumer.

If you calculate your profit, you find that your nominal profit has doubled since you have twice as much money coming in and the costs are twice as high, as well. But when you, the owner, pay doubled rent, purchase gas for twice as much and pay your doubled phone bill, you can buy exactly as much stuff as before. Your real reward for producing a pizza is exactly the same as it was before. This means that if inflation is spread evenly over all goods, so that each price increases by the same percentage, inflation does not affect production decisions.

Unanticipated Inflation

Suppose you had huge inventories of cheese when the inflation hits, so you will not have to buy more cheese for a year. That means that while pizza restaurants without these inventories must spend twice as much for cheese, you do not. This does not mean that your cost of producing pizza is lower, due to inventories. Here is why. Previously it took $1 worth of cheese to make a pizza, but now it takes $2 worth. Note, however, that an alternative to using cheese to make a pizza is to sell the cheese, and cost is the foregone value of the best alternative sacrificed. Previously, to make a pizza you had to forego selling the unused cheese for $1 (so the cheese cost was $1). Now, to make a pizza you forego selling the unused cheese for $2 (so now the cheese cost is $2).

Though the cost of your pizza is not lower because of the inventory, your wealth is higher. If you had, instead, signed a year's contract to buy cheese at the old price, the result would be the same. So when inflation occurs, you would like to have already sunk your old fixed value dollars into those things which now have higher prices—whether goods, or contracted services, or currencies from countries that do not have inflation problems. Gold is often used to protect against inflation, as are commodities like wheat, rice, and beans because their prices go up, along with inflation.

Loans work in this way, as well. In the same way that a contract to buy from a supplier at the old, low price, causes you to gain wealth and the supplier to lose wealth—if you have taken out a loan, before inflation occurred, you gain from the inflation, while the lender loses. For instance, if this year you take out a loan at 5% interest for $20,000 and buy a car, with payments of $400/year. If prices double next year—inflation is 100%—your car payments are in inflated dollars. Your wages rise along with inflation, so your monthly payments fall in real terms to $200/year. The lender, though, wishes it had not made the loan, and wishes you would pay off at once, before the value of dollars falls any more. If they expect inflation will stay at 100%, they will charge 105% for any new loans that others take out.

If everyone had anticipated the inflation, the cheese supplier would have demanded a higher price and the bank would have demanded a higher interest rate. But *with unanticipated inflation, borrowers gain and lenders lose—in fact, everyone who has a contract to pay with inflated dollars gains, while those who receive the inflated dollars lose. Also, those who are saving dollars lose.*

Banks quote a **nominal interest rate**—the rate that is advertised, which shows up on your financial statements. But banks formulate their nominal interest rate, based on what they expect inflation to be, aiming for a particular **real interest rate**. So if the bank expects that inflation will be 4%, and they desire to make 3% over and above inflation (the real rate), they charge a nominal rate of 7%. For loans with minimal risk, the real interest rate, the nominal rate minus the expected inflation rate, is about 2-3%.

The higher the risk of non-payment, the higher the real interest rate. Home loans are usually seen as less risky than credit card debt or other consumer loans, because there is a real asset—the home—that is good collateral, so their interest rates are only a bit higher than the "minimal risk" 2-3% rate. Loans with this kind of asset backing are called **secured loans**. Credit card interest rates are much higher, both because there is usually nothing backing the loan—that is, they are **unsecured**—and are higher because it costs the company much more to administer the credit card, whose payments vary and charges continue to pile up and be paid off.

Uneven Inflation

Inflation is not as smooth as in the pizza place example. Some prices rise more than others. Perhaps the price of housing is rising faster. This would make builders more interested in building houses.

The pizza place example used inflation that was spread evenly over all goods the economy—all prices doubled. *As long as all prices rise or fall by the same amount and inflation is anticipated, inflation has no effect on the economy.* It is as if now $2 is worth only $1, but since all prices rise, we receive $2 for each $1 we previously were paid, and everything we buy costs two times as much (gasoline that originally costs $3/gallon now costs $6/gallon).

The previous section dealt with unanticipated inflation. Now, consider inflation that is not perfectly anticipated <u>and</u> is not spread evenly over all goods in the economy—some prices rise a lot, some rise a little, some do not change, and some fall.

Two problems develop. The first is just that with uneven inflation, we do not know the real worth of goods. Wendy's finds that their beef supplier wants to raise prices. Wendy's does not know if this because of inflation or because the beef producer is just trying to chisel away some of Wendy's profits under cover of the uncertain inflation. A more fuel efficient restaurant cooker is on the market, but Wendy's does not know the future price of fuel, compared to the outlay on the cooker, because of the uneven inflation.

So we have a terrible problem in the market economy. In order for firms and consumers to produce and consume efficiently in a healthy spontaneous order, they need prices to tell them the about scarcity and about others' preferences. But with prices uneven and uncertain, they cannot make efficient decisions. This can cause less business to be done and for unemployment to accompany the inflation.

The second problem with uneven inflation involves the formation of bubbles in the economy. We have seen how money creation by the Fed results in more spending. There are more dollars sloshing around in the economy. Those dollars go somewhere, as people invest them and consume. These dollars may go into the stock market. They may go into commodities like wheat, rice, and beans. They may go into housing. This raises prices in some parts of the economy, "blowing up a bubble" somewhere in the economy, though it is difficult to identify where the bubble is or how big it is.

As Fed-created dollars pour into an economic sector, for instance, into housing, construction companies think that this new spending on housing is real, driven by the usual markets in which people save and invest in order to create value. More construction workers get hired and more homes are built. But, consistent with the equation of exchange, the central bank eventually sees an *overall* inflation developing and must stop creating money or further destabilize the economy. When the money creation stops, there are no extra funds to purchase many of the newly built houses, so they sit empty and construction workers are unemployed, along with lumber mill workers, surveyors, plumbers, and electricians.

The idea that money creation fuels inflationary bubbles, which burst and cause unemployment, was formulated by the Austrian economists Ludwig von Mises and Freidrich Von Hayek. Today in the economics profession the "Austrian school" uses a method of analysis practiced by many economists who are not necessarily from Austria.

Austrian economists view the overall spontaneous order of the market—based on tastes, knowledge, and scarcity, all connected by prices—as stable. In order for the entire economy to be destabilized, something must go wrong with the connections—something must go wrong with prices, in general. The thing that all prices have in common is the money supply, so the Austrians say that errors by central banks must be the root of all destabilization in the economy.

The Inflationary Tax

Money greatly lowers transactions costs, making trade easier, which means that individuals can create more value and have higher standards of living. Even in small populations, such as prison camps, we see goods evolving into money. Commodity money needs no central bank to oversee its creation, but fiat money does. However, central banks often try to create prosperity by creating money, though economists as far back as Adam Smith understood this to be futile in the long run—since wealth is mainly in the goods and services which we are able to use.

Here is how the central bank uses money creation, attempting to assist the state's spending, to the detriment of the economy. The state often spends more than it taxes, so it borrows from private citizens, from companies, and from other governments by selling its bonds to them. If a central bank, such as the Fed, attempts to assist the state in its borrowing by purchasing debt in return for dollars, we say they are **monetizing the debt**. Tin pot dictators directly monetize the debt by printing bonds and selling them to their relatives across the street at the central bank for newly minted currency. In highly developed nations the central bank may indirectly monetize the debt by purchasing billions in previously sold government bonds, from the public, using newly minted dollars. This means that there are people holding lots of money, who make good customers for the state to sell more bonds to.

This money creation causes inflation, which destabilizes the economy, but *inflation assists the state in financing its borrowing*. Recall that with inflation, borrowers gain and lenders lose. So, today the state borrows $100 billion dollars and, with the help of the central bank, creates inflation. With higher prices and wages, all forms of tax collections rise, making the state more able to pay the debt. So the state repays those who trusted it enough to lend to it with inflated, weaker, dollars, hurting those lenders. When the state creates inflation in order to reduce the value of its debt, it is said to impose **the inflationary tax**.

The term "printing money" too kindly describes the beginning of the money creation process. When the central bank of a developed nation buys $100 billion in bonds, they do not actually print currency. Since most money is electronic, the central banker pays for bonds by simply adding to the individual's bank account balance with a few strokes of a keyboard.

Tap, tap, tap. "There's more money in your account."

HISTORICAL INFLATION

When gold was used as money there was no general inflation or deflation over hundreds of years. With fiat currency, not backed by gold, central banks continuously create money, causing a strong long-run upward trend on prices. During the gold standard period, the average inflation rate was near zero, varying between -3.84% and 2.46%. During Fed's reign, dollar prices have averaged 4%, varying between -1.7% and 9.7%, according to Michael Bordo's data, which extends to 1979. http://www.econlib.org/library/Enc/GoldStandard.html [reference]

The following illustration is from Bordo's seminal paper on the gold standard. http://research.stlouisfed.org/publications/review/81/05/Classical_May1981.pdf [reference]

These are US prices from 1800 to 1979. During the Civil War, starting in 1860, the government began to issue greenbacks that they would not exchange for gold. In 1879, the government began to convert greenbacks to gold, upon demand. Considering only the years in which gold was the standard of exchange, ignoring the greenback years, the overall trend in prices was slightly downward—nearly perfectly stable. The Federal Reserve System was created in 1913 and, leaving out some of the story, prices were unstable for a time, but eventually began to march ever upward under the guidance of the Fed.

Figure 7.1

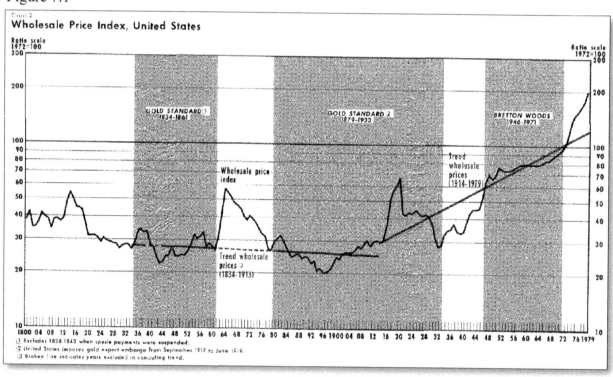

If we examine recent *inflation*, the percentage change in the price level, we get the following picture.

Figure 7.2

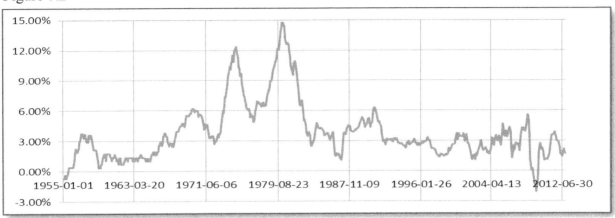

The inflation values are calculated using the CPI data at the St. Louis Fed's website, which is an excellent central source for economic data.

http://research.stlouisfed.org/fred2/series/CPIAUCSL?cid=9 [reference]

In the latter 1960s, Milton Friedman strongly cautioned the Federal Reserve Chairman that he was monetizing the debt created by the Vietnam War and by President Johnson's expansion of social welfare programs labeled "the war on poverty." Friedman's predictions of inflation came true during the late 1960s and early 1970s. As inflation destabilized the economy in ways the Austrian economists had identified, unemployment rates rose. This was met by more government spending and more monetization of the debt, which locked Fed chairmen in a destructive cycle that was eventually ended by Federal Reserve Chairman Paul Volcker in the early 1980s after inflation rates had spiked as high as 15%. When Volcker tightened the money supply, a short, deep, recession followed.

After Volcker, inflation moderated *to around 3% per year, which many now view as normal inflation.* But this causes prices to double about every 24 years, meaning that an individual's savings and retirement accounts are worth half as much after that time—recall that savers are lenders, who lose, due to the inflationary tax. Under stable prices, this would not happen.

Credit Markets

Direct Finance

Greg and Tom paused their game and Greg answered the door. Jen said, "Can we talk outside?"

Greg told Tom, "Be right back," and shut the door behind them.

Jen put her hand on his shoulder. "You're my last hope, hon, I have three car payments left and I'm behind on all of them. Can I borrow fifteen hundred dollars? I can pay you back when my tax refund comes in next week."

"Why can't you just pay then?" he asked.

Jen's voice quavered. "They're coming to take the car tomorrow afternoon and if I don't have it, they take it and I lose everything I paid on it. I've been paying for years. I can't lose it now."

Greg bit his lip. He should just say "no." This always turned out bad.

As he hesitated, Jen said. "My dad won't help, and my mom can't right now. She's way in hock. If I don't have the car, I can't get to work or to school. Please, Greg. It will only be for a week."

It would leave him with maybe $40 for the rest of the week. He let out a breath and nodded. "Yeah. OK. Come over tomorrow morning and we'll go to the bank."

A week later, Greg spent his last dollars on gas on the way to work. At work, Jen didn't mention the loan. His cereal would last him for two days, but the milk might only last for one.

The day after, his battery was dead. He got a jump and the auto parts place tested it and said it needed replacing—$110 for a new one. They charged the battery and he made it to work.

He joined Jen behind Ramona's Pizza while she took her smoke break. "Jen, I hate to bring it up, but I'm tapped out and I need a new battery. Did your tax refund come in?"

"Oh," she said, "that's terrible. How much will it cost?"

What difference did *that* make? "Over a hundred bucks. I hate to ask."

"Oh, OK. All the battery places will be closed by the time we get off work. I'm spending the weekend with some friends at Tech, but when I get back, I'll get you the hundred bucks."

"Do you know when your refund is coming in?"

She took a drag. "It came in two days ago. But it was just $1,200. And I had to spend $200 already and I need some for this weekend. We get paid on Wednesday, and I can probably get it all to you then.

He controlled his breathing. "Jen, I'm out. Nothing. I need a battery and I've got to buy food, and plenty more. Let's go to an ATM after work, and you can give me $300. I think that's the most they let you withdraw at one time. Tomorrow morning, you can get me another $300, then you can pay me the rest on payday."

Her cigarette tip burned orange as she drew a deep drag. "Fine," she said, spitting out the word.

He shook his head and walked through the back door. As the door closed, he heard her say, "Jerk."

DIRECT AND INDIRECT FINANCE

Read Bastiat, Chapter 11: Thrift and Luxury. http://www.econlib.org/library/Bastiat/basEss1.html [essential]

When asked "who are the suppliers of loanable funds," people often reply, "banks." But banks are not the true suppliers of loanable funds because nearly all the money they lend was first saved by someone with an account at the bank. The true suppliers of loanable funds are consumers and businesses that save. Banks are intermediaries—middlemen.

In credit markets, people trade money back and forth through time. Savers (lenders) are paid for delaying consumption until the future, by borrowers, who wish to consume or invest more in the present and will later pay for that privilege—the price they pay is **the interest rate**.

Direct Finance

With **direct finance**, a borrower deals directly with the lender, as Jen and Greg did, above. Businesses and governments who "sell bonds" to consumers, businesses, and governments, also are engaging in direct finance. Those who buy bonds are lending to the government or corporation they bought the bond from. Here is the structure of a government bond.

> Bond
>
> This seller will pay
>
> $1,000 to the buyer
>
> On January 5, 2020

This is how US government bonds look. Someone buys the bond, then can redeem the bond at a later date. The date that the payment will be made to the lender is called **maturity**. The value paid at maturity—the $1,000—is the **face value**. This bond is called a **zero coupon bond**, like all US government bonds and some corporate bonds, since the seller makes no interest payments. The reason someone would purchase such a bond is that they buy it at a bond auction for less than $1,000. For instance, if you were willing to pay $900 today to receive $1000 in one year, that would mean the interest rate on the bond was about 10%. Note that a zero coupon bond does not directly pay interest—it's just that you can redeem it for more than you paid. In January 2014, the interest rate on US Government bonds with a maturity in 5 years was about 1.5%.

Many corporate bonds also make interest payments twice per year until maturity, so the bond above would also have an interest rate quoted on it—the **coupon rate**.

Indirect Finance

When individuals and businesses use middlemen, such as banks, for borrowing and lending, they are engaging in **indirect finance**. From Bastiat's chapter 6, we learned that middlemen are paid because they add value. If they were useless, then no one would pay them. Just as in production, financial intermediaries, such as banks, are paid because they provide value to consumers and businesses. Imagine if you wished to save $10,000 and earn interest, but did not want to use a bank. You would encounter problems that a bank would have mitigated. Financial intermediaries such as banks,

- **Spread the risk of non-payment.** If you lend to a borrower, you may be repaid zero. But since banks make thousands of loans, most of which will pay, it is extremely unlikely that you will lose everything.

- **Develop comparative advantages in credit evaluation and collection.** If you advertised on Craigslist that you wanted to lend $10,000 you would likely have little way of evaluating potential borrowers. Also, if you loan to someone who does not repay, it will be expensive for you to take them to court to get the money back. But banks evaluate borrowers every day, have lawyers on retainer and have experience in getting borrowers to pay.

- **Divide denominations of loans.** You might find someone who wants to borrow $4,500 of your $10,000, then find someone who wants to borrow $8,000. Banks take deposits from many savers, pool them, and can lend different amounts, depending on the borrower.
- **Match time preferences.** You may wish to lend for 1 year, but find someone who wishes to borrow for 3 years—or for 6 months. Banks' constant churning of deposits and loans match up savers' and borrowers' time preferences.

SUPPLY AND DEMAND FOR LOANABLE FUNDS

The interest rate is the saver's reward for waiting to consume and the borrower's cost of consuming or investing early. With higher interest rates, the greater rewards encourage more saving—a larger quantity of loanable funds is supplied. But with higher interest rates, the higher cost of early consumption and investment discourages borrowing—a lower quantity of loanable funds is demanded. So supply and demand have their usual shapes, as below.

Figure 8.1

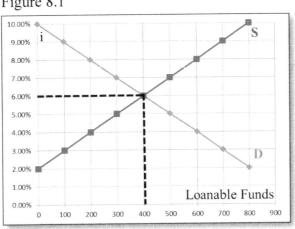

Here, borrowers and lenders are satisfied with the amount of funds they exchange, $400 billion, at an interest rate of 6%. As with any supply and demand analysis, borrowers would prefer lower rates and lenders would prefer higher rates. Tests of large financial markets have found them to be highly efficient, reaching • equilibrium quickly in the absence of government intrusion in the market. If the government enacted a **usury law**, which puts a price ceiling on interest rates, it would cause a shortage in the market if the ceiling was below the equilibrium interest rate. For instance, if the government capped interest rates at 5% there would be $200 billion shortage of funds. Consumers would find it difficult to get car loans, for instance.

Different loanable funds markets have different characteristics, as briefly mentioned in the chapter on money. Loans to the US government usually have the lowest interest rates—***about 2.25%. Mortgage loans have low interest rates—about 4%. Credit card rates are high, since the loans are not secured by property and have high administrative costs due to high default rates and unpredictable increases and decreases in the loan amount.

If the public decides to save more, the supply of loanable funds increases, which lowers interest rates, encouraging investment. Below, rates fall to 5% and $500 B is borrowed and saved.

Figure 8.2

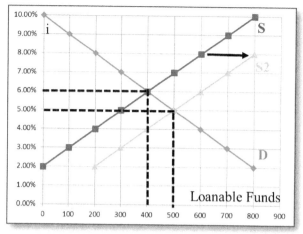

If people decide that the future is bright and their incomes will be high, their demand for loans increases, which raises interest rates and raises the amount saved and borrowed.

Government in the Market for Loanable Funds

There are two more players in the market for loanable funds besides companies and people who wish to save, consume, and invest. As discussed previously in the section on exchange rates and in the chapter on money, the US Federal Reserve creates money. Also the US government is a major borrower that has a huge impact on the loanable funds market.

In the chapter on money, we discussed how the Federal Reserve might create money in order to stimulate the economy and reduce unemployment. On the graph above, the new supply of loanable funds curve might come about due to this money creation process. The lower interest rates encourage investment. However, the chapter on money explained that while an increase in investment that is caused by savings, can produce goods that the savers may later consume—an increase in investment caused by an increase in money creation is only sustained by more money creation, inflating a bubble. Eventually the central bank must stop creating money as inflation mounts higher, which bursts the bubble, causing widespread unemployment.

The other large player, the US government, borrows, increasing the demand for loanable funds. In the graph below, the equilibrium amount of funds loaned (found on the horizontal axis) is $400 B. Then the government decides it needs to borrow $300 B, so the demand for loanable funds shifts right by the $300 B as shown.

Figure 8.3

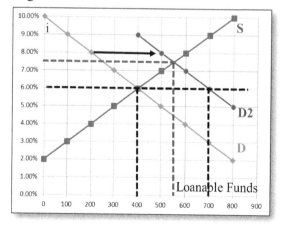

However, the new equilibrium amount of loanable funds is not $700 B. It is $550 B, as shown by the vertical purple dashed line. What happened to the other $150 B? As the government demands more funds, it drives up the interest rate. Funds that investors might have loaned to Apple, Microsoft, or Walmart, by buying their bonds, instead go to the government. And at the higher interest rate—7.5%—some businesses no longer want to borrow for investment in plant and equipment and some consumers no longer want to borrow for consumption or housing. When an increase in government spending is financed through borrowing, private spending decreases due to rising interest rates—this is called **indirect crowding out**. Bastiat's central thesis—that when government spends, private markets spend less because their ability to spend is taxed away—is called **direct crowding out**.

VALUE IN CREDIT MARKETS

Many in the public view credit markets as unproductive—simply moving money around. But, as Chapter 4 makes clear, trade creates value.

Suppose an individual can open a hot dog stand on a great street corner, greatly improving his ability to create value—his income—except that he does not have $5,000 and two months' salary to give him time to make it work. The individual can save, at interest, and open the stand later, giving up a higher income during that time or can borrow at interest and begin making a higher income now. If the hot dog stand is really a good idea, the individual can increase his value creation abilities now and can pay interest out of those increased value creation abilities.

Financial trades may create value because of differing abilities—one partner has ability, motivation, fewer other opportunities, but little capital while the other partner is lacking either ability or motivation, or has better other opportunities, while having the wealth necessary to acquire capital, so one partner finances while the other partner manages.

An extreme example of a financial transaction that creates value is the **leveraged buyout**, where a firm borrows in order to purchase another firm, then immediately sells the firm in whole or in parts. Here is an example. An entrepreneur sees that a certain corporation's stock can be purchased for $10 million, but it owns assets, such as oil leases, worth $14 million. How could this happen? It must be the case that the corporation's management of the assets is terrible, so that they can only turn $14 million in oil reserves into a $10 million expected lifetime profit. The acquiring firm borrows short term, buys for $10 million, and sells the oil leases for $14 million.

The lenders get a piece of the profit, as interest, as does the acquiring firm. In the media, this is portrayed negatively, since the old company ceases to be. However, consider what will now happen to the valuable oil resources. A buyer who was willing to pay $14 million for them will likely use these resources better than the old company, creating more jobs, producing higher quantities of valuable oil. The acquiring firm has moved resources from low valued uses to high valued uses.

So, in a manner of speaking, finance moves money around—but it does so to move resources around, from less valued uses to higher valued uses, resulting in an increase in the wealth of a nation and nearly always creating employment opportunities.

Bankruptcy and Value

When firms cannot pay their obligations and cannot borrow more to pay, they may declare bankruptcy, triggering a legal proceeding. A firm whose value is negative—owes more than it owns—is **insolvent**. But a solvent firm might be forced to declare bankruptcy because it is **illiquid**—cannot pay its immediate obligations. Consider the following firm:

Table 8.1

$1 million in cash
$2 million in assets easily convertible to cash
$4 million in payments due
$6 million in assets not easily convertible to cash
$3 million is owed to the firm by others who will likely pay
$5 million in long term debts

If this firm can simply slow down payments to creditors, it can receive payments, sell some easily convertible assets, and/or use cash to pay its creditors. But if the payments are badly timed—perhaps the managers were counting on a large cash payment that was not made—the firm might have to slow down the process by one variant of bankruptcy. This firm is solvent—overall it owns or is owed $12 million and owes only $9 million. With more in long term debts, the firm would be insolvent. In fact, a firm might have more in long term debts and less in short terms debts, so that it is liquid—can pay in the short term—but are insolvent—they owe more than they own.

In some bankruptcies, parts of the firm are sold and the creditors are paid. For instance, Hostess, the makers of Twinkies, declared bankruptcy, held an auction and sold the right to make Twinkies for over $400 million. Without buying that brand name, other firms could make cream-filled snack cakes—they just could not call them "Twinkies."

If General Motors, which had a terrible illiquidity problem in 2008, had declared bankruptcy, they might have sold auto plants to other companies. These plants would have continued making cars, possibly under other brand names, but likely under the same brand names. And most of the workers hired by the new owners would likely have been previous workers. The new owners would not have operated the firm identically to the old owners, but the facilities would not disappear with a bankruptcy and neither would all the jobs. Perhaps Toyota could have used the facilities in a more efficient way than General Motors. So bankruptcy contributes to economic health by moving resources to more productive uses, creating value.

Sometimes the creditors do not receive all they are owed, since the firm may owe more than it has. Courts are supposed to follow the **absolute priority rule**, by which the creditors are ranked with regard to how long ago the company became indebted to them, then every penny is paid to the "senior" debt, before any less senior debt is paid. Then every penny is paid to the next senior debt class, and so on. The stockholders—the owners—are last on the list. In the General Motors case, the state entered the process, threatened senior creditors, and handed payoffs to less senior creditors who were political friends. This violation of basic property rights will likely suppress lending in the future, since creditors' rights may not be honored in bankruptcies of large firms.

Thinking Exercise 7.1: Credit, Savings, Spending

Read Bastiat Chapter 9: Credit
Review Bastiat Chapter 11: Thrift and Luxury
http://www.econlib.org/library/Bastiat/basEss1.html [essential]

- Bastiat says in paragraph 1.230 that the state's actions raise the rate of interest. Explain how, using the supply and demand for credit.
- Is there a reason for thinking that lending the plow to James will have any better results for the economy than lending it to John?
- What interest do the taxpayers have in the credit example regarding the plow?
- True, false, explain: The Bastiat example of the plow does not apply to our economy.
- Is there any difference between the Bastiat plow example and the last chapter's Austrian theory of bubbles? Explain.
- In Bastiat's example of Mondor and Ariste, how does Ariste's savings harm the economy?
- Paragraph 1.263 says, "the wise spending of Ariste will go on increasing year by year." Since Ariste is receiving value, it must come from somewhere. Where does this value come from? Is someone getting poorer so that Ariste can get richer?
- Several taxes on savings went into effect in 2013—one from PPACA, the health care law, and the others from the expiration of tax cuts passed in 2001. *True or false, explain:* Since these taxes only affect money that was not being spent anyway, they will only take from one group and give to another group, without affecting overall economic activity.

THE 2008 CRISIS AND THE PROPOSED REMEDY

Cause and Crisis

The 2008 crisis was triggered by a collapse in housing prices. But triggers are not causes—the fall in housing prices had causes that extend back to the Great Depression.

During the Great Depression, large errors in Fed policy caused a banking crisis. Fannie Mae (the Federal National Mortgage Association) was created to restart lending on housing after the crisis. Fannie Mae was privatized in the late 1960s as a secondary market for home lending—purchasing safe home loans that banks had made, which encouraged banks to lend more. Freddie Mac was created at about this time to compete with Fannie Mae.

Fannie Mae and Freddie Mac, the FMs, bought loans from banks, received payments from homeowners and sold bonds to the creditors which paid interest from the homeowners' loan payments. This allowed individuals to invest in the overall real estate market by purchasing FM bonds without going through the trouble of buying and selling individual properties. The process is shown in the following figure.

Figure 8.4

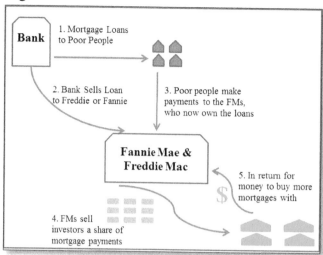

Though the bonds said they were not guaranteed by the government, everyone but a few US legislators who received campaign contributions from the FMs knew that the government would pay if the giants could not. Since the only loans the FMs would buy were backed by real estate and were made to reliable borrowers, things went well for a while.

In 1977 the **Community Reinvestment Act** became law, which instructed banks to make loans to poor people, who could not get home loans before, because they could not pay. No penalties were levied on banks that did not follow these instructions. Later, banks who wanted to merge with other banks were denied by federal regulators because they had not made enough community reinvestment loans, so banks began to make some loans to poor people. In the early/mid 1990's the US Department of Housing and Urban Development (HUD) directed the FMs to purchase loans that banks made to risky borrowers who could not meet the old standards—**nonconforming loans**. This passed the risk of making loans to poor people from banks to the FMs. Throughout the 1990s and into the 2000s, HUD raised the target ratios of nonconforming loans. Here is a statement on the subject from HUD. The comments in brackets are mine.

"Over the past ten years . . . Fannie Mae and Freddie Mac have been a substantial part of this 'revolution in affordable lending'. During the mid-to-late 1990s, they added flexibility to their underwriting guidelines [*bought loans made to people who were not good credit risks*], introduced new low-down payment products, and worked to expand the use of automated underwriting in evaluating the creditworthiness of loan applicants [*stopped emphasizing creditworthiness*]. . . . [*the FMs*] are increasing the flow of credit to underserved borrowers [*poor people*]. Between 1993 and 2003, conventional loans to low income . . . families increased at much faster rates than loans to upper-income . . . families."

In the early 2000's top financial journalists at the *Wall Street Journal* exposed the problems at the FMs, but influential senators, such as Chris Dodd, and congressmen, such as Barney Frank, defended the FMs when the administration attempted to make the FMs file financial reports similar to those required of most financial companies.

During the early 2000s the Federal Reserve greatly increased the money supply, lowering interest rates, fueling even more home loans. With the FMs making huge profits from serving poor people, private markets tried to compete by purchasing low quality loans, insuring them with the AIG insurance corporation, and selling bonds backed by the mortgages and insurance, just like the FMs.

While the Fed's low interest rates fueled increases in housing prices, when a poor borrower defaulted, the lender repossessed the house and sold it for more than it was purchased for, protecting the investors who bought the bonds. When the Fed began to lower the money supply to keep from causing large inflation, they found that they had helped to inflate a housing bubble, consistent with the Austrian school's story. Housing prices fell, revealing that the industry was massively overbuilt—with loans to borrowers who could not pay.

Fannie and Freddie failed and could not pay their bondholders. The state used nearly two hundred billion taxpayer dollars to pay off those who owned FM bonds. AIG failed and the state used taxpayer dollars to pay those who had insured their mortgage bonds with AIG. Two major investment houses failed and major banks failed. Taxpayers paid off all of the money that the failures owed to their creditors.

The bailouts were orchestrated by the president of the New York Federal Reserve Bank, Timothy Geithner, alongside Federal Reserve Chairman Ben Bernanke, and Secretary of the Treasury Hank Paulson. During this time, they collaborated on a proposal that congress hand them $700 billion to buy all the bad mortgage backed bonds. The proposal was called TARP, the Troubled Asset Relief Program. Eventually congress passed the TARP legislation, but Paulson handed the billions to banks, instead of using them to buy the bad bonds. The seven largest banks received $25 billion each, including Wells Fargo, who did not need the money and tried to refuse it.

Paulson and the regulators would not let banks refuse the funds, since if some banks took the money and others did not, it would point out to the public which banks were weak, prompting customers to withdraw deposits from banks that took TARP funds. Later, other banks, such as BB&T, tried to refuse funds that they would be forced to pay interest on, but they were threatened by the Fed and the treasury department. http://www.nytimes.com/2009/08/02/business/02bbt.html?pagewanted=all&_r=0 [reference] Eventually the funds, passed to aid banks and financial houses, were even used to bail out failed auto companies, such as General Motors.

Proposed Remedy

Congress's proposed remedy for financial crises, the Dodd-Frank bill of 2010, was 2,300 pages that:

- created new government regulatory agencies,
- created new regulations, and
- directed regulators to write additional regulations.

As of May 2014, regulators were still in the process of writing the regulations that were authorized four years earlier. *** What Dodd-Frank does **not** do is restrict the FMs in any way. Recall that Dodd and Frank were the top recipients of campaign contributions from the FMs.

Here are a few of the many things the Dodd-Frank bill does:
- **Established the Financial Stability Oversight Council**, headed by the Secretary of the Treasury, that is supposed to identify **systemic risks**—risks to the entire financial system. The chairman of the Fed, a major cause of systemic risk in the early 2000s, is a member of the FSOC. FSOC can designate financial institutions as "too big to fail"—Systemically Important Financial Institutions (SIFIs), guaranteeing that they will be bailed out if needed, causing the market to pour more money into them. In addition, if the FSOC actually breaks up financial institutions, the regulators, themselves, may be introducing huge systemic risks because regulators who have outlandish authority can make outlandish mistakes.
- **Instituted bailout insurance**—financial institutions pay into an insurance pool. If a major financial failure occurs, the insurance pays the cost. As mentioned in Chapter 2, a major unintended

consequence of insurance is that those who are insured have more incentives to take risks, hence financial markets will likely take inefficient risks and need more bailouts in the future. Since the past is the best predictor of the future, taxpayer funds will likely be used when the insurance pool runs low.

- **Created the Consumer Financial Protection Bureau to regulate consumer credit.** A major early target of the CFPB is the credit market for the poor—pawn shops and payday loan companies. Since the poor are risky borrowers, forcing companies that serve them to act as if they are serving the middle class and rich is ending the legal credit market that the poor use, driving them to loan sharks. The CFPB is nearly beyond control by elected representatives. It receives its funding through the Fed, independent of congress. Only its head, designated by the president, must be approved by the senate.

The proposed remedy for the crisis amplifies the problems that caused the crisis. The FMs are untouched by the legislation. Bailouts went from being an occasional illegitimate practice, to a practice that is written into law. Consumer credit, which did not cause the crisis, is under assault. And government regulators, who could not spot previous problems as they developed, now have authority to decide which firms live and which firms die.

Current Credit Market Problems

Besides the Dodd-Frank law, government bureaucrats now behave as if they forgot everything that happened in the crisis.

- The US Justice Department is now forcing mortgage companies and banks to resume making loans to poor people.
- The Department of Housing and Urban Development has approved Fannie and Freddie offering low down-payment loans to attract low income borrowers.
- With the help of the Justice Department, Fannie and Freddie have sued banks who sold them the bad loans that the Department of Housing (HUD) insisted they buy. The FMs official position is that their highly skilled financial analysts were tricked by fraudulent banks, although the truth is that the FMs eagerly bought loans they knew were risky. Two banks have settled for a total of $10.5 B to end the Justice Department's targeting.
- The Fed and the US Treasury Department have purchased over $200 billion of FM securities in order to supply them with cash.

AFTERMATH OF THE 2008 CRISIS

The 2008 crisis brought together the value destruction that accompanies government insuring of loans (as Bastiat warned against in his chapter on credit) and Austrian business cycle theory on how Fed money creation inflates bubbles. The bubble burst, followed by the weakest recovery since the Great Depression. Here is a summary of the economy as of this writing.

The Labor Market

An unemployment rate of around 4%-5.5% is considered normal. Unemployment reached a high of 10% during the recession. It was 5.9% in September 2014. http://research.stlouisfed.org/fred2/series/UNRATE [reference]

As the data make clear, the unemployment rate was at its highest level since the 1982 recession, during which Federal Reserve Chairman Paul Volcker tightened the money supply in order to end the inflation caused by previous Fed money creation. Six years after the 2008 crisis, the unemployment rate is much lower than at the peak. It has now nearly fallen to the high of the last recession, which began in the year 2000.

Figure 8.5

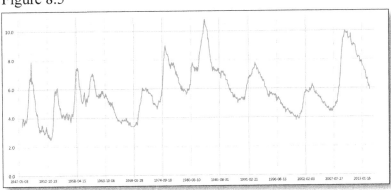

Though some new jobs have been created since the 2008 crisis, an important reason that unemployment has recently fallen is that people are only counted as unemployed if they are looking for work—and millions fewer Americans are looking for work. The graph below shows that the percentage of Americans who are looking for work is the lowest it has been in over three decades.

Figure 8.6

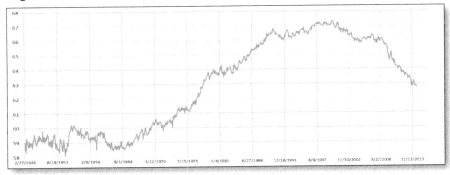

A major change from previous recessions and recoveries can be seen in the average duration of unemployment, in weeks. As shown below, previously, the average unemployed person was out of work for about twenty weeks, at maximum, but during the recession and through the recovery this average was about forty weeks—twice the previous high, since the Great Depression, only recently falling to 31 weeks. The likely cause of this increased duration of unemployment is the state's extension of unemployment benefits. Previously, unemployment benefits only lasted for approximately 26 weeks—half a year. But during the crisis and recovery, congress and the president extended unemployment benefits to as much as 99 weeks—about two years. This will likely result in lower employment in the future, since the long-term unemployed often do not seek further employment after their benefits expire. For those who want to learn more, the following link discusses the topic. http://econlog.econlib.org/archives/2012/09/how_much_do_99.html [reference]

Figure 8.7

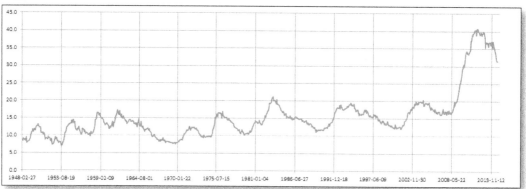

Economic Growth

Economists make clear that wellbeing is best measured by goods and services. A healthy economy's increased production of goods and services—**economic growth**—is at least around 3% per year. In recessions, economic growth is negative. To recover from a recession and eliminate excess unemployment, economic growth must be higher than 3%. For instance, the recovery from the 1980s recession saw growth rates of around 8%, as pictured below. In the most recent quarter (not pictured), growth was -2%. ***

Figure 8.8

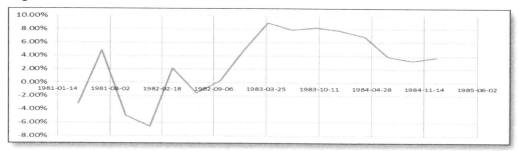

Contrast the growth in the 1980s recession/recovery with the 2008 recession/recovery, through January 2014. Instead of the high sustained growth rates of 8% in the 1980s, the 2008 recession and recovery only managed to exceed 3% during four quarters. The minimum growth rates during the 80s recovery are around the maximum growth rates of the 2008 recovery.

Figure 8.9

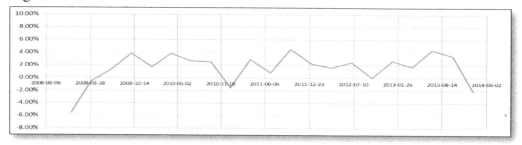

Inflation and Potential Inflation

The 1980s recession was caused by Paul Volcker's "inflation fighting" contraction of the money supply, followed by normalization. The 2008 crisis was triggered by a necessary contraction of the money supply, accompanied by bad housing policies by government, followed by a huge monetary expansion to fight the recession. Real estate's bursting bubble caused overall prices to fall, though a higher money supply contributed to inflation in much of the rest of the economy. But since housing is such a large component of the CPI, the deflation in housing during and after the crisis masked the inflation in the rest of the economy.

Figure 8.10

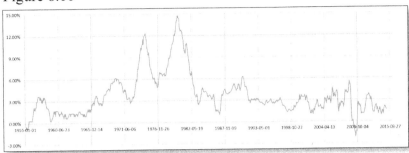

The picture below is the M1 money supply, which is given in billions—so 1,500 is really $1.5 trillion. See how money growth accelerated from 2008 through 2012. http://research.stlouisfed.org/fred2/series/M1 [reference]

Figure 8.11

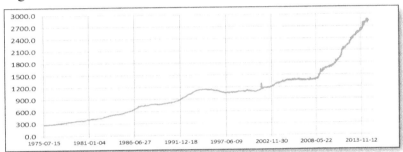

This growth in the money supply gives fuel for inflation, as predicted by the simple quantity theory and by monetarism. However, a more ominous picture emerges when one considers the potential inflation that the economy could manufacture if a robust recovery took hold with increased borrowing. Recall that a bank can lend its excess reserves—reserves beyond those which are required—so that excess reserves throughout the banking system represent the potential lending power of all banks.

Historically, the banking system's excess reserves ranged from fractions of a billion dollars up to two billion dollars. If one looks closely at the graph below, one can see the month of September 2001, when a major terrorist strike on a financial center froze billions of dollars in place, taking excess reserves from $1.2 billion up to $19 billion (an all-time high). But excess reserves fell back to $1.3 billion in October as the banking system quickly recovered from the event.

However, since the crisis, the Fed's expansion of the money supply has increased excess reserves from $1.8 billion in August 2008 to $2,517 billion in July 2013. The previous high of September 2001 pales in significance. Reserves are held in the banking system because Chairman Ben Bernanke began to pay interest on excess reserves. If Bernanke raises this interest rate too high, dollars flow into the banking system choking off a recovery or causing a recession. If Bernanke lowers this rate too much, the excess reserves flood the economy and cause the greatest inflation since the US Civil war. Given that these excess reserves are many orders of magnitude higher than traditional levels, top monetary economists cannot comprehend how the Fed can return to historical levels of excess reserves without causing a financial disaster.

Figure 8.12

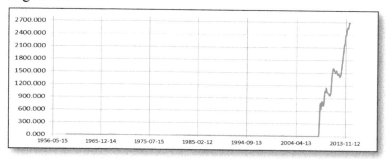

In conclusion, the previous financial crisis was caused by bad government housing policies, accompanied by rapid money growth. Congress passed Dodd-Frank, which amplifies the problems that caused the crash. Meanwhile, the Fed has tried to cure the problems with credit markets by rapid monetary growth, but this causes the potential for future disaster.

Output, Income, and Economic Growth

GROSS DOMESTIC PRODUCT

What We Count and What We Do Not Count

Recall that Adam Smith said, "the wealth of a country consists, not in its gold and silver only, but in its lands, houses, and consumable goods of all different kinds." Free markets work to maximize the wealth of nations through value creation.

- Some of this created value is consumed quickly—such as with strawberries.
- Some of this value is consumed slowly—such as with housing.
- And some value is saved.

In this chapter we study how much value an entire economy creates in a year. Since all value that is created benefits someone, the previous sentence could have read, "In this chapter we study how much income everyone in an economy earns in a year."

Note that income is not the same as wealth. *Wealth is a stock*—like a lake—your bank account balance, plus the portion of your car that you own, plus the portion of your house that you own. *Income is a flow*—like a river—how much your paycheck is. So income reflects value creation, while wealth reflects accumulated past value that has been saved.

In macroeconomics each unit of a good or service is valued at its price, not at the amount of gain to society from its manufacture, because we usually only have information on market prices, not on how much someone would have been willing to sacrifice or to accept. So, though the first slice of pizza on the graph below has a value of $4.00 to a buyer, and costs $1.00 to produce, creating $3.00 in social gain, in macroeconomics that slice of pizza's market value is $2.50, the price. We would prefer to measure social gain for each good and service produced, but must settle for the market price—which does reflect value and cost, though not as well as social gain.

Figure 9.1

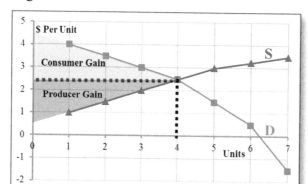

What we actually measure—the amount spent on the good in the market—is show below.

Figure 9.2

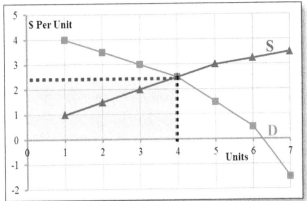

Since 4 units were sold at a price of $2.50 each, the market value of this good is $10.00. There are two differences between the two graphs above—the upper one which has what we would like to count and the lower which has what we actually count.

- The consumer's gain is missed in these actual calculations. Consumers are willing to pay more than the $2.50 for nearly every slice of pizza. There is no remedy for this problem.

- We count the pizza producer's costs for materials like flour, *as income*. Surprisingly, this is not a bad thing, because the cost of flour *is* income—for flour producer. But since we count the price of flour as part of the price of the pizza, we <u>should not count</u> the price of flour separately. We only count the prices of **final goods**—those sold to a final user, and not the prices of **intermediate goods**—those not sold to a final user.

So the amounts spent on pizzas and cars and sofas, etc., are added up, as in the table below.

Table 9.1

Good Produced	Amount Spent
Pizzas	$8 billion
Autos	$564 billion
iPads	$2 billion
Sofas	$5 billion
...	...

Gross Domestic Product (GDP) is the current market value of all final goods and services produced within the country's borders in one year.

GDP tells us how big an economy is. Here is the list of countries, ranked by GDP.

http://databank.worldbank.org/data/download/GDP.pdf [essential]

You can see that the largest GDP of any single country is the US, with over $16.8 trillion*** of production, for 2013. Only China approaches this. Countries with lower GDPs are not necessarily poorer. For instance, Chile is ranked 38th on the GDP list, but is ranked 60th in terms of population, while Hong Kong is ranked 39th, just one below Chile on the GDP list, but is ranked 101st in terms of population. Since Hong Kong has about the same GDP as Chile, but Chile has a much higher population, the average individual in Hong Kong produces more valuable output than the average individual in Chile produces.

GDP does not count all transactions that take place because there are no records or market values for some production, and because other transactions would cause double counting. For instance,

- Production of underground illegal goods, such as heroin, is not counted because we have insufficient records.

- Production of underground legal goods—working off the books—is not counted because we have insufficient records.

- Production that does not enter markets, such as being one's own cook, maid, or car repairman, is not counted because we have insufficient records.

- Sales of used goods are not counted since the original sale was counted. *But services of middlemen in selling used goods are counted.*

- Financial transactions—sales of stocks, bonds, and the like—are not counted because either; most are not original sales, so they are like used goods, or, if they are original sales, used to finance the acquisition of capital, we count the capital, so we don't count the funds raised to purchase the capital. To do so would be like counting the $20,000 you paid for the new car and the $20,000 car loan you received—the output involved is only $20,000, not $40,000. However, services of financial professionals are counted in GDP, just like with used goods

- We do not count government **transfer payments**—taking from one person and giving to another, but not in return for any good or service—such as social security, unemployment insurance checks, and food stamps.

- We do not count the value of leisure—though we count tickets to Six Flags, MMO subscriptions, and other market activity that accompanies an individual's leisure time.

- We do not subtract **bads**—unwanted phenomena such as disease, crime, and garbage. Keynesian economists assert that bads may, paradoxically, increase GDP because we pay to lessen their effects—such as hiring policemen to combat a new crime wave. Keynesians are correct in pointing out that the crime wave would make us worse off. However, *Keynesians err in thinking* that GDP will rise, since people must give up goods in order for government to hire policemen. Hence, people have fewer pizzas and more policemen, so GDP does not rise. Different outputs are produced, as happens in Bastiat's broken window story.

This course uses **the expenditure approach** to discuss GDP, which is the usual approach that is discussed on the news and in the most referenced government reports. With this approach, we add up the current market values of all final goods and services. If someone paid $20,000 for a new car that was produced this year, we add $20,000 to GDP. If someone paid $25.00 for a steak dinner, we add $25.00 to GDP.

However, government statistics are actually calculated using **the income approach**, which adds up all the payments to factors of production—the wages, interest, rents, and profits—generated by production. Government uses this method because they gather these data as people pay taxes.

Here is why the two approaches are equivalent. When a consumer purchases a car for $20,000, the entire $20,000 is income for someone in the economy. Some of the $20,000 goes to the auto dealer, some goes to auto company stockholders, some goes to the auto workers, some goes to steel workers, some goes to accountants, etc. A sale of $20,000 generates income of $20,000. Each penny is a gain for someone. So in macroeconomics, **Income ≡ Output**. The identity relationship, denoted by the ≡ symbol, says that though income and output are defined in different ways, they are equal.

The Expenditure Approach

The expenditure approach breaks GDP down by the four groups who spend on final output.

- **Consumption**—spending by consumers on nondurable goods, durable goods, and services. Durable goods are those which last for at least a year.
- **Investment**—spending by business on capital (plant, equipment, tools, etc.), changes in business inventories, and spending on new residential housing. Note, this does not mention stocks or bonds.
- **Government Purchases**—spending by all levels of government on goods and services. Note that transfer payments do not fit this definition.
- **Net Exports** = Exports - Imports. Note that this makes it seem as if "Exports, good. Imports bad," which is contrary to what we learned in the trade chapter. However, both imports and exports are done by those who are making the economy better off, so the trade chapter is correct.

Here are the percentage shares of GDP that each makes up—the sum is 100%. In the past, investment was the second largest component of GDP, but now government purchases is.

http://www.bea.gov/iTable/iTable.cfm?ReqID=9&step=1#reqid=9&step=3&isuri=1&903=14 [reference]

Figure 9.3

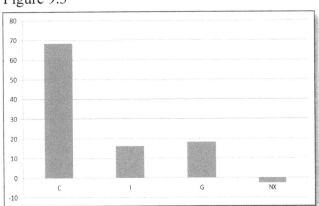

Thinking Exercise 9.1: Leftover Lawn Mower

- Murray, Inc. manufactured a lawn mower on February 14, 2011.
- Walmart bought the lawn mower on April 1, 2011, for $1,000, planning to sell it to a customer.
- Walmart sold it for $1,000 to a customer who uses it to mow her lawn on March 15, 2012.
- Which two GDP concepts conflict with regard to the lawn mower's history?
- In which year and in which category of GDP is the lawn mower counted?
- If Walmart sold the mower for $1,500, how would the lawn mower affect GDP?

Real GDP

In calculating GDP, we use current market prices to reflect the values of the goods and services. A Mercedes has a value of $115,000, which can be compared to a dozen donuts, which have a value of $7.00. Without prices, we could not be specific about how much more the car was worth, compared to the donuts. However, as previous chapters made clear, inflation causes money to lose its function as a store of value. It would be best to measure value in units that are not distorted by inflation.

The most logical way to approach the problem might be to construct a price index, as in a previous chapter, to adjust the GDP numbers. The Bureau of Economic Analysis performs an equivalent, but different analysis. They derive **Real GDP**, which is what GDP would be if prices had remained the same as they were in a base year. In this way, Real GDP reflects only quantity changes, and not price changes.

When we look at how well the economy is doing over time, we always use Real GDP to remove the effects of inflation and only look at how many goods and services we are producing.

However, if we are comparing values at a single point in time, we might use GDP (which we could call nominal GDP or current dollar GDP). For instance, the graph above shows the percentages of GDP devoted to consumption, investment, government spending, and net exports. We can easily derive these percentages using current prices, since we would be dividing today's consumption at current prices by GDP at current prices. If we convert both of them to real values, we get the same answers. Similarly, we often hear that the national debt is bigger than GDP—the debt is about $17.8 Trillion and GDP is about $17.3 Trillion.*** We get good information from these numbers without converting both to real values, where the real debt would still be larger than real GDP, because you would divide both numbers by the same prices.

ECONOMIC GROWTH

Economic growth is the percentage change in Real GDP. It is the best measure of whether an economy is getting better or worse. Economic growth does not tell you how well people in the economy are doing. People in China are mostly poorer than people in the UK, but China's economy is growing faster than the UK economy. After WWII, the US economy grew quickly. Today, the economy is not growing as quickly, but we eat more and better food, live in bigger and better houses, and drive bigger and better cars, than after WWII. At any time, though, we would prefer more economic growth to less—that is, we want the economy to improve.

Since the number that we derive for Real GDP depends on the base year, and is, thus, arbitrary we never have reason to look simply at Real GDP numbers, themselves. We only look at growth rates in Real GDP, which are the same, no matter which base year is used. It is like measuring a child's height, we could say it is 3 feet, 36 inches, or .914 meters—but if, as an adult, the child's height increases to 6 feet, that is still a 100% increase, no matter how it is measured.

A picture of real GDP follows. Though many who are asked would say that our economy swings wildly up and down, the data reveal that we generally grow. For most of the years, we do not see an actual decrease in real GDP from year to year, though sometimes growth slows. During periods of slow growth, new jobs are not added to the economy fast enough to keep up with our growing population, so more people will be unemployed.

Recession

Two successive quarters (three month periods) of negative economic growth is called a **recession**. Throughout this data series, we spent 9% of our time in recession and 91% of our time not in recession. So it is not the case that the economy is flat, or is in constant decline, or that it swings wildly up and down. It mostly grows.

Figure 9.4

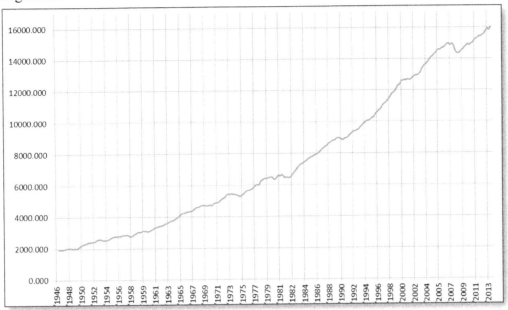

Real GDP using 2009 as a base year

Here is how the health of the US economy is generally seen to relate to economic growth. The numbers are not exact, but generally reflect views of economists.

Table 9.2

If Growth is:	The economy is considered:
Over 3.0%	Strong
2.5-3.0%	Acceptable
2-2.5%	Weak
0-2%	Sick
Less than 0%	Horrible

Some view high growth as dangerous—possibly inflationary. But, as discussed in the chapter on money, inflation is caused by increases in the money supply, not by increases in output. If the central bank performs a helicopter drop of dollars, we may see high short run growth, which is followed by long run inflation. Economic growth is not a cause of the inflation—it is a short run result of money growth.

Below is a graph showing quarterly economic growth, beginning with the lead-up to the financial crisis of 2008. Note that since the negative growth rates began, the positive growth was rarely at least 3%, which we classify as strong. Over the 20 quarters, a great deal of economic growth was sick or acceptable. Without strong growth, jobs were not created quickly enough to satisfy an expanding population, so unemployment stayed high and many gave up looking for jobs. Because the years from 2008-2013 were weak, the young, who have only been conscious of the economy during those years, have a distorted view. Mostly, the economy grows—but not lately. In the third quarter of 2014 the economy grew by 4.9%, and four of the last five quarters have been strong. After six years of weakness, we may have begun a strong recovery.***

Figure 9.5

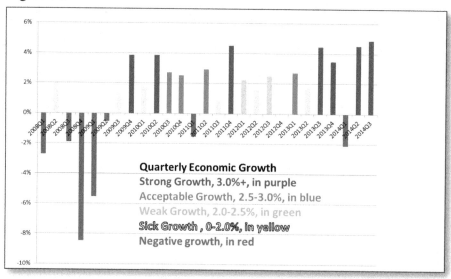

Growth in Real GDP: First quarter 2008 to third quarter 2014.

<u>**Business Cycle Language**</u>

The language that we use to describe the ups and downs of economic activity is a kind of shorthand, based on a stylized view. **The business cycle** describes the ups and downs of the economy.

As seen on the following graph, an increase in Real GDP is called an **expansion**. At the **peak** of the business cycle, Real GDP is at a temporary high. When Real GDP falls, the economy is suffering a **contraction**. Two successive quarters of (three month periods) decline in Real GDP is called a recession. At the **trough** of the business cycle, Real GDP is at a temporary low. As Real GDP grows from the trough, a **recovery** is occurring. There is no specific length of time that a recovery must continue before we call it an expansion, though a usual guidepost involves unemployment falling to pre-recession levels.

Figure 9.6

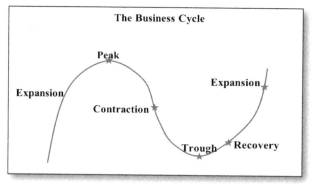

Some use the language incorrectly, for instance, saying that the US was in recession from 2008 through 2013, because unemployment was so high. In truth, the US was in a sickly recovery that could not bring unemployment down to its pre-recession levels. Below is the tale of two recoveries. The horizontal axis is the quarter number. The blue line is economic growth following the 1982 recession, while the red line is economic growth following the last recession. Both lines show the quarters coming out of the recession, but following the 1980s recession, growth is very strong—over a year at 6% or more—while following the 2008 recession, growth is mostly sickly, at around 2%. A growth rate of 3% is considered strong, but coming out of a recession, more is needed to quickly return the economy to normal.

Figure 9.7

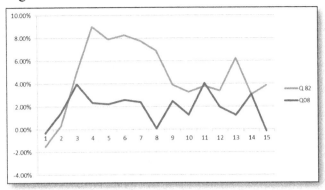

Recovery From the 1982 recession and from the 2008 recession

PER CAPITA GDP

Recall that:

- GDP tells us the size of the economy. To compare to other countries, we need to convert using some sort of exchange rate. We also use GDP for comparisons with other current dollar measures of economic and government activity.
- Real GDP is used to examine economic growth over time, since it removes the effects of changing prices.

Neither measure illustrates the wellbeing of the people in a country. For this, we use **Per Capita GDP**—GDP divided by the population. With this measure, combined with an exchange rate conversion, we can compare the wellbeing of people in different countries. To look at the growth in wellbeing over time in a single country, we use Real Per Capita GDP. Below is Real Per Capita GDP in the US in 2011 dollars. As with Real GDP, we see a strong growth trend. We see more places that level out, which might be expected because the values are influenced by population growth, including immigration.

Figure 9.8

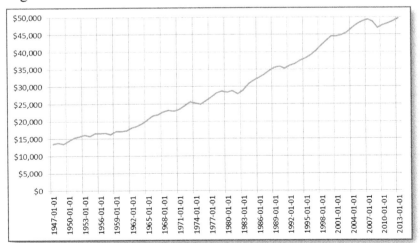

Real GDP Per Capita

Note that although poor immigrants may lower Per Capita GDP, immigration does not represent a loss in wellbeing. By way of analogy, when a child gets on an elevator full of adults, the weight of the average person falls, but the adults do not get any skinnier. As seen in the trade chapter, more and varied resources create value. In fact, if one country's Real Per Capita GDP is greater than another's, when an above average person in the poor country moves to the rich country, this could lower both countries' Real Per Capita GDPs. And a below average person moving from the rich country to the poor country could raise both countries' Real Per Capita GDPs.

Per Capita GDP Data

Per Capita GDP is the best measure we have, though it is not perfect because it does not take account of the distribution of income within a country. So some countries with relatively small populations that have a few multi-billionaires, along with mostly poor people, have high Per Capita GDP. These are the exceptions and are usually easy to spot. The World Bank's estimates of Per Capita GDP have the US as the major industrialized country with the highest Per Capita GDP—about $50,000. The countries that have higher living standards are small, such as Qatar, Liechtenstein, and Singapore.

http://data.worldbank.org/indicator/NY.GDP.PCAP.PP.CD?order=wbapi_data_value_2012+wbapi_data_value+wbapi_data_value-last&sort=desc [reference]

The following table summarizes the data, mostly for major industrialized countries. However, it also includes other countries of interest to the US. The average US resident is about 25% better off than the average Canadian, which is significant, given that for an individual working at a job, a 25% raise is large. It is about what the average US resident spends on all transportation from buying and insuring the car, to buying the gasoline. Some might say that Canadians might still be better off, since they have socialized medicine. However, expenditures on health care, which is part of government purchases in Canada, are included in their GDP, so this is not a source of the difference.

Table 9.3

Country	Per Cap GDP
United States	$51,800
Australia	$43,700
Canada	$42,500
Germany	$41,200
United Kingdom	$37,500
France	$36,100
Japan	$35,100
Italy	$33,100
Russia	$23,500
Chile	$22,400
Mexico	$16,700
China	$9,100
Egypt	$6,600
India	$3,800
Pakistan	$2,700
Congo	$415

Economic Freedom and Wellbeing

A major reason that incomes are higher in some countries than in others is greater economic freedom, as shown by the Index of Economic Freedom, cited in Chapter 2. The US has fallen in the IEF rankings for seven consecutive years, indicating that the nation is moving away from the path of economic growth.

In evaluating any measure of economic health, both the level of economic achievement and also economic growth must be considered. The average US resident would not want to trade living standards with the average Chinese resident. But, if China grew at an amazing long-term rate of 10% per year, while the US grew at a satisfactory 3% per year, China's populace would be, on average, as well off as the US populace in 23 years. This would not be disastrous, since the average US resident would be nearly twice as well off as compared to the average US resident is today. Even if China pulled even with the US, this does not make Americans worse off—Americans' meals would not taste any worse simply because people in China were eating the same types of meals.

Economic growth is not only related to the level of economic freedom, but also to the change in economic freedom. If a state that has no economic freedom grants a small amount of economic freedom, it might experience huge economic growth, raising the population from horrible living standards to less horrible living standards. But high economic growth does not mean the slightly more free state has found the correct policies, only that it has found the correct direction for economic policies.

For instance, if the state moves from a policy of no person being able to open any business to a policy that only men over fifty years old can open a business, the initial growth rates due to the expansion of freedom might be huge, compared to mature countries where men and women, young and old, can open a business. But that does not mean that the particular policy is correct—only that the direction is correct. So as a country like China chooses more economic freedom, they move in the correct direction, but that does not mean that every policy they have—from limited internet access, to the one-child policy, to severely limited rights to own a home, to their still huge government ownership of much of the means of production—is good.

Some segments of the US news media mistake growth due to a government choosing a correct direction for policy with growth due to having correct policies. In addition, Chinese students are taught incorrectly that their new, robust growth is due to correct policies, not from less incorrect policies than previously prevailed.

BUREAU OF ECONOMIC ANALYSIS DATA

The Bureau of Economic Analysis compiles official GDP data for the US Their most recent news release is at http://bea.gov/newsreleases/national/gdp/gdpnewsrelease.htm [essential].

Thinking Exercise 9.2: Reading the BEA Data

If you have learned the material thus far, you can interpret nearly all of the BEA GDP report.

- Which economic statistic does the BEA see as most important?
- How did the economy perform in the most recent quarter?
- How did the economy perform in the quarter before that?
- Would you generally expect the final quarter of the year to have more economic activity or less?
- Find each of the components of the expenditure approach to GDP, previously listed in this chapter. How healthy was each component?
- What was nominal GDP—called "current dollar GDP"?
- Look at the growth in current dollar GDP and the growth in real GDP. What is the difference between the two? Why is there a difference?

Labor Markets

FREE MARKETS

Labor Demand

People start businesses and hire others in order to make themselves better off. People work for others in order to make themselves better off. They interact in labor markets.

In the simplest case, an employee adds to production of a good and the firm sells the good. The **Law of Diminishing Returns**, outlined in Chapter 1, said that for any particular plant size, as more labor is used, the extra output that an employee can produce declines at some point. So the value of hiring an extra worker falls as more employees are hired. In the table below, the marginal product—the extra output that an employee can produce—falls.

Table 10.1

Employees	Marginal Product of Each	Total Output of Employees
1	38	38
2	30	68
3	23	91
4	18	109
5	12	121
6	6	127
7	0	127

The extra output is not the true value of the employee to the employer—it is the extra revenue that comes in from selling that extra output. Suppose in the above table that the output sells for $10 each. The value of each employee is given below.

Table 10.2

Employees	Marginal Value of Each Employee (VMP)
1	$380
2	$300
3	$230
4	$180
5	$120
6	$60
7	$0

We could re-label the column above "**Value Marginal Product**" (VMP), which is the Marginal Product of a worker multiplied by the price of the output. Using marginal analysis, outlined in Chapter 1, the owner will hire the employee if the value of the employee, in terms of extra revenue coming in to the firm, is as least as great as the cost of having the employee. Suppose the numbers above are daily production by laborers whose wage is the national average—about $20/hour—$160/day (http://bls.gov/news.release/ecec.nr0.htm [reference]). The firm would find it profitable to hire the first worker, since that worker produces 38 units of output per day—enough output in a day that when the owner sells the output for $380, it will pay for the wages of $160/day. We can continue this analysis to find that the second employee is also profitable to hire, and the third and fourth—but not the fifth, who can only produce 12 units of output, which sell for $120—not enough to pay the $160 wages.

But if the owner hires four employees, the owner has forgotten something. The analysis done in the previous paragraph assumes that wages are the only labor cost. The news release above reveals that in addition to wages of about $20/hour, firms pay an extra $10/hour in benefits, including the cost of complying with labor regulations, health care coverage, contributions to a retirement plan, social security contributions, workers compensation (a federal insurance program), and unemployment contributions. This brings the total labor cost to about $240/day, which means that the employer should not hire the third and fourth workers—only the first two. Higher wages or higher non-wage benefits cause employers to hire fewer employees.

If the total labor costs per employee could be cut to $100/day, the firm would hire five employees. If total labor costs per employee rise to $400, the firm uses no hired labor and might have to shut down. Note that for every labor cost, we look at the Value Marginal Product to figure out how many employees to hire. This means that *the VMP is the demand for labor*. It slopes downward, like other demand curves, due to the Law of Diminishing Returns.

Labor Supply and Market Equilibrium

Labor supply comes from employees' willingness to work for various rewards. For higher wages and benefits, more people are interested in working and those who work are interested in working more hours.

As outlined in Chapter 1, the shape of this curve depends on the alternative uses of the employee's time and the principle of optimal arrangement. Spending time on the job nearly always involves doing things one would rather not do, so employees will not work unless they are compensated. Other things equal, more tedious jobs require higher compensation be paid in order to keep employees on the job. As employees spend time on the job, they *first* sacrifice the least valuable other uses of their time. In order to work even more, they must sacrifice more valuable alternative uses of their time, according to the principle of optimal arrangement. So an employer must pay higher wages and benefits in order to get employees to work longer. This means that the labor supply curve is upward sloping, as seen below.

The labor demand curve comes from employee productivity and the product price, while the labor supply curve comes from the employee's willingness to work at various wages and benefits. Together, labor supply and demand yield an equilibrium in the market depicted below—$15/hour, with five units of labor. Perhaps the five units of labor represent 500,000 people working in a country.

Figure 10.1

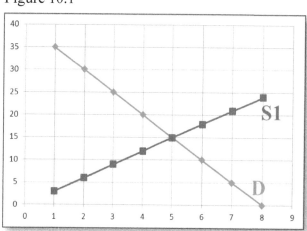

Each labor market is different, since landscapers, engineers, and cooks have very different skills and competitive conditions. But each market works in a similar manner, as employers compete to hire the best workers available at the price and as employees compete to find the best jobs, given their levels of productivity.

Employees would rather be paid millions of dollars for doing little work, and employers would rather employees work hard for zero wages and benefits, but neither can or will cooperate to give the other exactly what they want. Their differences are settled in a market that is so orderly that most of the time job offers are simply made and accepted or rejected, without a great deal of arguing and fighting, in the same way that consumers and convenience store owners do not argue and fight over the price of gasoline.

If, in the above market, workers have other non-labor opportunities, such as are provided by social welfare programs, labor supply falls. This results in less employment and higher wages. Though these high wages may sound attractive, less employment means less is being produced, overall. But if less is being produced, overall, the nation *cannot be better off even with the higher wages*. The key is that, in effect, some of the higher wages and benefits are going to the beneficiaries of the social welfare program.

Figure 10.2

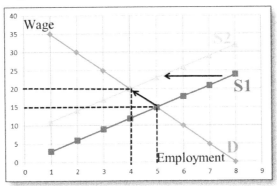

Suppose, instead, the government places taxes or higher regulations on employers that raise labor costs. This causes the demand for labor to fall, as seen below. This lowers employment and wages. The law of unintended consequences often applies to these situations. When legislators desire to improve conditions for workers they often raise labor costs, resulting in lower wages and less employment. Social security taxes lower the demand for labor, as does raising the cost of legally firing an employee, as do Workers Compensation programs, which provide for injured workers.

Many European countries impose even more restrictions on firing than in the US. *The Wall Street Journal* reported on labor law in Italy.

> "Today, if you want to fire a person, he goes to court and the judge forces you to take him back," explains Ms. Novellone [an Italian manufacturer]. Under [proposed] reforms, the courts could still force employers to rehire fired workers if they don't agree with the cause for dismissal. But during hard times, businesses could in future lay off workers for the low price of up to 27 months' severance pay . . . "This would be a big improvement," says Ms. Novellone. "If you can fire people, it means you can also hire people."   *Jolis*

http://online.wsj.com/article/SB10001424052702303404704577308014134697828.html [essential]

Figure 10.3

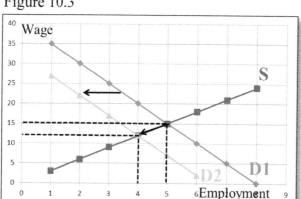

Improving Labor

Since employees are paid for productivity, anything that raises productivity increases output and, hence, income. Education and training may improve productivity, building the individual's **human capital**, raising the demand for the individual's labor.

However, another theory of why education improves employee incomes is that employers wish to hire individuals who will show up, work, and can learn—and that anyone who completes a degree or a certification program has signaled that they will do these things. **Screening theory** says that education and training may be valuable to the individual, not because the training increases productivity, but because it points out which employees will be good.

Under both theories, education should be demanding. However, under human capital theory, it matters what the subject matter is, though, while under screening theory, the subject matter is not of interest. As long as earning a degree requires mental and physical effort, the signal is valuable.

Individual productivity is improved, and, thus, income is also improved by access to capital, including information technologies. A worker with a bulldozer is more productive than a worker with a shovel. Hence, bulldozer operators are usually paid more than shovel operators. Some worry that bulldozers put shovelers out of work, but societies with more bulldozers are more prosperous than those with shovelers.

SPONTANEOUS ORDER, PLANNING AND MAKE-WORK FALLACY

Story: The Dark Bargain

I drank from her wooden bowl, cinnamon taste souring on my tongue. My body hummed. Numb. The crone with the crumpled face said, "Now you won't feel a thing."

She hunched forward, leaning every ounce of her undernourished body onto the knife until its burnished edge chopped through the knuckle at the base of my little finger. Blood pulsed out the stump until she seared it with a glowing iron from her brass bowl filled with coals. The smell and sight of the sizzling stump tightened my throat. I would have lost my dinner, if I had eaten.

"Is that . . ." I started. "You'll bring *him* now? I have nothing else to give."

She tossed the finger in white hot coals and it cooked there. She said, "I can't imagine what the old man will tell you that is so important." She chanted, whined, clicked her tongue, retched, hissed, until the smoke from the coals took shape—a wispy face regarded me.

She had done it. I had paid dozens like her before. My heart thudded against my ribs. Tears formed. I addressed the blank eyes, "Amos Weller, I'm your great great grandson, Pieter. I have to ask you something . . ."

"Pieter?" the wavering smoke whispered. "Keep me with you. I beg you. I am in torment below."

"Yes, Grandpa, anything. But I need to know—in Grandma's diary, she spoke of your dark bargain." Sweat rolled down my face. I panted, trying to slow down so he would understand me. I did not know how much time was left. "The bargain frightened her—sacrificing your soul in favor of your descendants. I am your descendant, but I have found no favor in life. I scratch and claw for everything I get. I have taken to selling illegal drugs to finance my search for the answer to this question. How am I favored by your bargain?"

"You don't know? Keep me here. I will tell you." I could see lines of torment etched in his smoky image—marks of agony of spirit, drawn by a century of torture. He said, "I sold my soul to darkness, that all my descendants might have a better life than I. That they might excel where I failed."

"But I have not exceled at anything."

His blank eyes stared. "You do not excel? Tending your beasts? Weeds and pestilence banished from your lands? The finest crops growing to left and right of any plow guided by your hand?"

My voice deserted me. The crone said, "You have your answer."

I coughed away the lump in my throat. "Your blessing was that my manual labor in agriculture would be rewarded? Men no longer guide plows. Megacorporations with massive machines, genetically engineered seeds, and chemicals produce food, without farmers putting a hand to the plow. No."

He whispered, "I gave all that I had for it—that is your blessing."

I bolted upright, crying. With my good hand I flipped the table backward, upsetting the brass bowl, spilling coals around the crone's shack. I walked forth, weeping, as the flames crackled behind me.

☼☼☼☼☼☼☼☼☼☼☼☼☼☼☼☼☼☼☼☼☼☼☼☼☼☼☼☼☼

Science fiction writers predicted that we would all use energy from the sun, lasers, flying cars, pocket communicators, computers, space ships, and robots. At this point, they were absolutely right about pocket communicators and computers, and were partially right about solar energy and robots. They could not know which would happen first or would be the easiest. They envisioned every home with a huge room for massive computers. They envisioned robots doing housework, but those are only in the early stages. Solar energy is still much more expensive than energy from fossil fuels and is used mostly as a luxury item by the wealthy.

We cannot know what the future will be like, which means we do not know what the labor market of the future will be like. The German and Spanish governments placed large bets on solar and wind energy, but are now paying so much for them that they have scaled them back. In these ways, human central planners who claim to know the future, move resources away from high valued uses toward into low valued uses, making us worse off, since they cannot solve the calculation problem that the Austrian economists of the 20th century outlined.

The spontaneous order of markets adjusts to a technology such as railroads by killing some jobs, but creating more efficient, high value jobs. As transportation costs fell, more trade was possible. The market for every producer's goods expanded. And more production became possible since resources could be inexpensively moved to newly built factories. Many who had lost jobs making wagons found better jobs because trade and production possibilities expanded. And many people who had difficulty finding work at all before railroads were built found that the demand for labor was higher and wages were higher because of the new technology.

In addition, planners boast about jobs created by government spending in directing these resources. For instance, the US Environmental Protection Agency brags that for "every 10,000 tons of solid waste going to landfills, 1 job is created. That same amount of waste—kept out of landfills—can create 10 recycling jobs or 75 materials reuse jobs." http://www.epa.gov/region9/newsletter/feb2011/greenjobs.html [reference] The public can see jobs that are created from inefficient uses of resources, but they cannot know which efficient uses of resources—which jobs—were destroyed. The idea that jobs have value, regardless of whether the labor actually creates value, is called **make work fallacy**.

Though we cannot predict the future, we can predict the effects of some policy changes. In the skilled labor market below, the equilibrium wage is $15/hour. If the state requires that no employee be paid less than $20/hour, (that is, imposes a **minimum wage**) more potential employees will begin looking for jobs (the quantity supplied would rise to 700,000), but employers would not offer as many jobs at the higher wage (only 400,000). This would cause unemployment that the workings of supply and demand would not cure. A minimum wage of $20/hour in a market for unskilled labor, where wages are much lower, would have drastic consequences. But that is exactly what was proposed in March of 2013. (http://www.nationalreview.com/corner/343240/elizabeth-warren-asks-why-isnt-minimum-wage-22-hour-eliana-johnson) [reference]

Figure 10.4

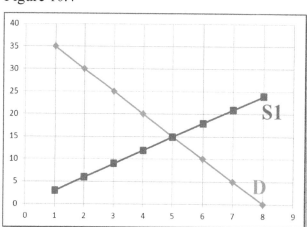

> **Reading Exercise 10.1:** Bastiat Chapter 2: The Demobilization http://www.econlib.org/library/Bastiat/basEss1.html [essential]
>
> - Does Bastiat think military spending is wasteful? Explain.
> - How does Bastiat answer the charge that a decrease in military spending results in troops being unemployed?
> - What does Bastiat assume about free markets for labor?
> - What does Bastiat call "a dead loss for the nation?"
> - What does Bastiat say about maximizing the nation's profit?

LABOR MARKET STATISTICS

The Bureau of Labor Statistics (http://bls.gov) [reference] uses their **establishment survey**, in which they ask large businesses about how many employees are on their payroll, to measure the number of jobs the economy is creating. However, the establishment survey omits all self-employed persons or contractors, who do not appear on the company's payroll, but only as an operating expense.

The BLS **household survey** asks individuals about their employment status by telephone. From this, the BLS staff compiles the unemployment rate and other statistics. Here is the latest news release. (http://www.bls.gov/news.release/empsit.nr0.htm) [essential] In order to understand the news release, we should first review the BLS definitions. (http://www.bls.gov/news.release/empsit.a.htm) [essential] As of May 2014, these statistics were as follows. ***

Table 10.3

US Population	Approximately 315 million
Civilian Non-Institutional Population (CNIP)	Members of the population 16 years or older, not in the military, and not institutionalized. The reason that the military is omitted is that otherwise wartime makes the unemployment rate fall, making it look as if the labor market is doing well. About 248.5 million.
Employed (E)	Everyone who worked at least 1 hour for pay or profit in the previous week. Everyone who was not paid for working in a family business, but worked at least 15 hours at that business in the previous week. Everyone who missed regular work due to illness, vacation, strike, etc. About 146.6 million.
Unemployed (U)	Everyone who was not employed, but made specific, active efforts to find a job in the previous four weeks. Everyone who was waiting to be called back from a layoff. About 9.3 million.
Civilian Labor Force (LF)	Employed + Unemployed. About 155.8 million.

The unemployment rate is the unemployed, divided by the civilian labor force.

$Ur = U/(LF) = 9.3/155.8 = 5.9\%$ (note, some rounding was done).

Any unemployment rate over 5.5% is considered high. The highest unemployment rates since The Great Depression are around 10-11%, so we have seen worse. (http://research.stlouisfed.org/fred2/series/UNRATE) [reference]

Note that the labor force does not include the entire civilian non-institutional population. Some of those in the CNIP, but not in the LF include retired persons, teens who choose not to work, university students who choose not to work, stay-at-home dads and moms, some handicapped people, bums who live in the park, and bums who live in the basement playing *Call of Duty*. These people are counted as neither employed nor unemployed.

In the third paragraph of the BLS news release (linked above) you can see that unemployment varies greatly by age and race. A 21% teen unemployment rate is partially due to an increase in the minimum wage of 24% from 2007 to 2013. Currently, 2.3% of workers earn the minimum wage. However, it might be the case that many of the 21% of unemployed teens would work for less than the current minimum wage if it were legal to do so.

The Labor Force Participation Rate (LFPR) is the LF divided by the CNIP. It measures how many people are interested in holding a job.

$LFPR = 155.8/248.5 = 62.8\%$ (some rounding was done)

This is the lowest LFPR since the mid-1970s. (http://research.stlouisfed.org/fred2/series/CIVPART/) [essential] A falling LFPR reveals an economic/societal problem that the recent recession and sluggish recovery has accelerated. Some portion of the falling rate is due to the unattractiveness of work, compared to welfare alternatives. A large part of the recent fall may be due to a flood of applications for social security disability, not because of an increase in actual disabilities, but as a result of the poor labor market. Prior research has shown that someone who has stopped looking for a job for a year is unlikely to ever work again.

The LFPR for men has been falling for a long time, (http://research.stlouisfed.org/fred2/series/LNU01300001) [essential] while that of women, until the last recession was rising, but is now falling. (http://research.stlouisfed.org/fred2/series/LNS11300002) [essential] Compared to men, women are doing better in the labor force than ever. A recent survey revealed that young women (20-30 years old) had about 8% higher incomes than young men, with the Atlanta area yielding the largest differences—young women in Atlanta earned 20% more income than young men. Much of the increase in female earnings, relative to male, is due to education. In 1980, 40% of university graduates were female. Today 60% of university graduates are female. In addition, women marry later in life and bear children later in life than in 1980. (http://www.aei-ideas.org/2013/04/equal-pay-day-for-young-single-men-to-recognize-the-gender-pay-gap-in-favor-of-young-single-childless-women/) [reference]

Discouraged workers are those who have looked for a job at some time during the previous 12 months, but are no longer looking because they think no jobs are available. The employment news release (linked above) discussed them. They are not listed among the unemployed because they have not looked for a job in the past four weeks. Some fraction of discouraged workers have real unemployment problems, however, at some point, if one ceases to look for a job, we might classify their problem as a personal problem. Since the BLS cannot sort out which is which, they report discouraged workers separately.

In bad economic times, more workers are likely to become discouraged. But, note that as people stop looking for jobs, they are no longer counted as unemployed. In fact, if every unemployed worker became discouraged, the unemployment rate would be 0%—since no one is looking for a job. So in bad times, the unemployment rate understates the true economic problem. Similarly, as times improve, some discouraged workers begin to look for jobs again, causing the unemployment rate to overstate the true economic problem.

After one year, discouraged workers are no longer counted at all, except as members of the CNIP. So if economic times are especially difficult for more than a year, even the discouraged worker statistics fail to reflect the true economic problems. These considerations make changes in the unemployment rate sometimes difficult to understand. In April 2013, 73,000 jobs were lost, but 806,000 people left the labor force. This means that the entire decline in the unemployment rate (from 6.7% to 6.3%) was from short-term and long-term discouragement. We think of the unemployment rate as the one statistic that shows the health of the labor market, but we must always look deeper into the numbers.

This is also complicated by the fact that people leave the labor force for other reasons than discouragement—such as raising children and retirement. However, at the same time, young people enter the labor force. It takes about 250,000 new jobs each month to slightly lower the unemployment rate by adding jobs. It takes even more new jobs to significantly lower the rate.

A special unemployment rate known as U-6 includes people who have stopped looking for jobs and those who are part time, but want to be full time. U-6 was 12.3% in May 2014, while the quoted unemployment rate was 6.3%. (http://research.stlouisfed.org/fred2/series/U6RATE) [reference]

New claims for unemployment insurance are compiled by the states and collected by the Department of Labor on a weekly basis. The news media likes weekly numbers, since their business involves presenting new information. At first glance, one might expect that these new benefits filings would rise as unemployment became more of a problem, and would later fall. However, at some point, many of those who have become unemployed are either receiving benefits or have exhausted their benefits and cannot re-file. So as the unemployment problem continues we might see new claims fall because of exhausted benefits or continuing benefits, not because the economy is getting better.

In addition, politicians who wanted to seem compassionate extended the duration of unemployment benefits above the usual 26 week limit (half a year)—up to 99 weeks (two years) during the 2008-2009 recession/recovery. This further prevented the strong recovery one would see by encouraging some of the unemployed—those who, for instance, live with parents—to delay re-entering the labor force until their benefits expire. Casey Mulligan of the University of Chicago found that half of the increase in unemployment in the recession and recovery came from extending unemployment benefits.

(http://caseymulligan.blogspot.com/2012/11/recession-by-redistribution.html) [reference]

TYPES OF UNEMPLOYMENT/FULL EMPLOYMENT

Frictional unemployment occurs because of the normal workings of the labor force with people changing jobs and entering the labor force with the skills that will likely soon yield a job. If the BLS called you as you were moving from your old job to a new job, and you had not worked during the past week, you would be frictionally unemployed, though you had accepted a job. Similarly, a doctor who, in anger, quits a job working at the emergency room, and prepares to enter private practice is frictionally unemployed, as is a newly graduated medical student who is interviewing for jobs on hospital staffs and is nearly guaranteed to find a job. During good economic times people are more likely to quit jobs since they know jobs are plentiful—so frictional unemployment can actually rise during good times and fall during bad times, when people are afraid to quit jobs. Similarly, in good times, people are more likely to be able to get better jobs, so they are more likely to be frictionally unemployed.

Structural unemployment is a longer term problem which occurs due to changes in the labor force that render some skills obsolete. It may be due to changes in technology, to trade, or to changes in consumer tastes. For instance, in the 1980s oil prices collapsed, causing many oilfield workers to be structurally unemployed. Lower oil prices boosted economic activity, which raised overall well-being, but the skills that many workers possessed were no longer needed. The antidote to structural unemployment, in some cases, may be education and training. The state often proposes to train new workers, but the history of government training programs is terrible. (http://online.wsj.com/article/SB10001424053111904332804576538361788872004.html) [fun reference]. About the best the state can do is hand someone money to find training or education in the market, however, most of those who could benefit from such training have already acquired it.

Cyclical unemployment is what we usually think of as unemployment—it arises due to contractions that occur during the business cycle. With rising cyclical unemployment, politicians promise rationally ignorant voters that they can fix the unemployment problem by spending money. However, since people know their abilities and the local labor market better than national politicians know them, the economy could heal if people try to solve their own problems. The spontaneous order of the market, in which everyone pursues value creation, does not have coordinated failures across many firms and many markets. Research done by Austrian economists and the Chicago School shows that government errors are the best coordinator of market failures, so the state is often found to the cause of downturns in the business cycle. Here are some examples of government errors coordinating economy-wide failures, resulting in cyclical unemployment.

- The Great Depression began as a major blunder in monetary policy. It was prolonged by government policies that tried to control minute aspects of the economy, including the New Deal's destroying crops and livestock, wholly changing the monetary system from commodity money to fiat currency, unpredictably increasing taxes, mandating increases in labor costs, and criminalizing market competition. (http://www.cato.org/publications/commentary/how-fdrs-new-deal-harmed-millions-poor-people) [reference]

- The economic problems of the late 1960s began with the Fed's monetization of the US Government's debt incurred due to the Vietnam War and The Great Society's welfare programs. It continued through the 1970s and into the 1980s as monetary authorities switched from increasing the money supply in an attempt to cure unemployment to decreasing the money supply in an attempt to cure inflation caused by the former increases in the money supply. The state also increased its control of energy markets.

- Fed Chairman Paul Volcker's tightening of the money supply brought an end to the problems of the earlier decades, although it caused a deep, but short, recession.
- The 2008-2009 recession was caused by decades of government interference in housing markets, combined with Fed monetary growth of the early 2000s.

Full employment is said to exist when there is no cyclical unemployment. This means that a fully employed economy has some frictional and structural unemployment. The logic behind this is that healthy economies have frictional and structural unemployment, so we should not "count them against" the economy. Frictional unemployment is natural and is not problematic. In addition, an economy with no structural unemployment would not be growing and changing. That is, (1) if the economy is not leaving anyone behind, it is not moving and (2) if the economy is not moving, it is not healthy. Countries such as Somalia and Cuba likely have little structural unemployment, since their economies are stagnant. At full employment, the unemployment rate is approximately 5.5%. Typically, anything over 5.5% is seen as a cause for alarm. When the economy is at full employment, GDP reaches its potential, as shown on the production possibilities frontier in Chapter 3.

Though the news media often simply reports on unemployment rates as rising or falling, this chapter makes clear that there is often more to the story. One should consider whether the labor force is growing or shrinking, because unemployment can fall due to discouragement—and long term discouragement does not even show up in the data. Further, some are working fewer hours than they would like. U-6 gives us insight into these problems, but still does not reflect all the issues. Unemployment duration helps to capture an important aspect of the problem, but is influenced by unemployment benefits—obscuring whether the problem is one of markets or one of government. Finally, the labor market is much richer than can be portrayed in a graph. For many purposes, data on bank tellers should not be compared to data on genetic engineers.

Macroeconomic Adjustment

SAY'S LAW

In explaining how the economy adjusts to reach its potential, Jean-Baptiste Say first reasoned that when someone offers a good for sale in a barter economy, he must demand something in return. The good offered has a value and any reasonable person would demand something of at least equal value. Since the person's trading partner would also demand at least equal value, the market value on each side of the trade must be equal. **Say's Law** is, thus, *supply creates its own demand*. If you supply a good, you demand something of equal value in return.

In this way, there can never be an overproduction or an underproduction of goods. If you produce twice as much lumber as usual, it might be the case that the price of your lumber would fall, in terms of how much beef you could get per board foot of lumber. In this case, you might only get half as much beef. But it is still the case that supply brings forth an equal value of goods to trade, because, although the value of the lumber has fallen, there is more of it.

Say observed that in a money economy, however, something could go wrong with the above example. In a money economy, you might sell lumber for $1,000, then buy only $600 worth of beef, and save the extra $400. This would mean that there could be an imbalance between the overall supply and demand, so there could be an overproduction of goods—looked at another way, this would be an underconsumption of beef. But Say showed why his law would still hold.

Say, like Bastiat, observed that "to save is to spend." That is, unless one hides money under the mattress, it is spent by someone. Even in 1850, Say and Bastiat dismissed the idea that there was a great deal of money under the mattress—nearly all savings was in the banking system. And in loanable funds markets, the interest rate adjusts so that all saved funds are loaned out at the equilibrium interest rate—6% in the graph below. So Say observed that his law holds in a money economy because the interest rate adjusts to eliminate shortages or surpluses of funds.

Figure 11.1

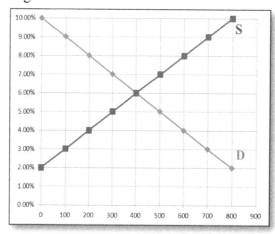

Suppose our lumber manufacturer, and many others, decide to save more. The old interest rate was 6% and at that rate, people wanted to save $400 billion. But now, they want to save $600 billion at the old 6% interest rate, as shown by the shift from S to S2 in the graph below. With a higher supply of loanable funds, interest rates fall until all the saved funds are loaned out—the rate falls from 6% to 5% and, at that rate, all of the decreased consumption, due to savings becomes investment and consumption fueled by borrowing.

Figure 11.2

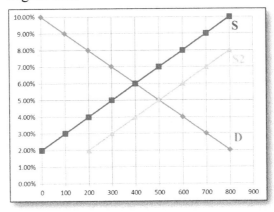

Hence, Say's Law, which relies on free market adjustments of interest rates, guarantees that there cannot be a general overproduction or underproduction of goods. Note that an overproduction of goods would necessitate that workers be laid off until the inventories were sold—that is, a recession would occur.

THE LINK BETWEEN THE LABOR MARKET AND THE OUTPUT MARKET

Like credit markets, labor markets also adjust to return the economy to equilibrium. The chapter on production developed the idea of combining resources to produce output and noted that if resources were fully employed then output was the highest possible—that is, a point on the production possibilities frontier. We can now call these points on the production possibilities frontier, where output is at its maximum given our inputs and technology, **potential GDP**.

Figure 11.3

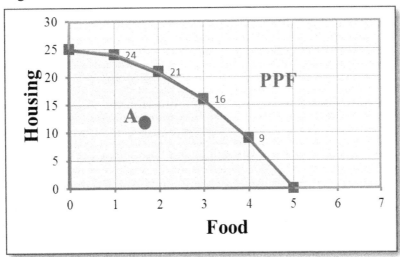

However, if output is below the PPF, that is, below our potential GDP at a point above, like A, there are unemployed resources. That is, workers are trying to find work, but cannot, so there must be a surplus of labor, as seen below. More labor is being supplied by workers than is being demanded by firms, meaning many workers do not have jobs, but are looking for jobs.

Figure 11.4

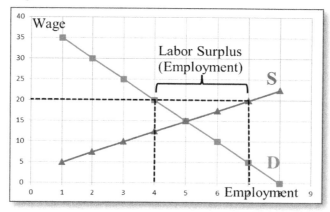

Early economists realized this link between potential output and unemployment and theorized that since *wages adjust to eliminate shortages and surpluses*, we must always be at our potential. That is, the situation above does not happen. However, some economists contended that there were times when we observe inventories building up, causing a general unemployment—that is, at least for a while there was a surplus of labor and we were below the PPF. They called this situation a "glut of goods," which we would call a "recession." So these economists reasoned that there was more to the story than free markets adjusting to maintain full employment.

Classical economists in the 1700s up to the early 1900s hypothesized that any gluts of goods happened because markets might, under some circumstances, not adjust quickly to huge systemic changes—such as earthquakes or war. Later this tradition was refined by the Chicago School as **real business cycle theory**, which said that much of the business cycle comes from real shocks to productivity. However, both the Chicago School and the Austrians also looked toward government as a creator of recessions, either through misdirection of resources because of regulation, due to a government laboring under the calculation problem, or through errors made in the money supply.

KEYNES' VIEW OF LABOR MARKETS

John Maynard Keynes, writing about The Great Depression, hypothesized that labor markets might not reach equilibrium quickly. So that if an imbalance in the economy gave us a labor surplus—that is, if a higher-than-equilibrium wage gave us unemployment—the wage may not fall quickly. Keynes said that unemployment would persist until something from outside the labor market changed.

Keynes' story begins with the economy at full employment, but then irrationally pessimistic feelings that he called **animal spirits** spread throughout the economy. This causes people to want fewer goods and services (demand falls) causing prices to fall. To explain Keynes' logic, it is helpful to remember the "pizza place example" from the chapter on money. If all prices are cut in half, including pizza prices, cheese prices, electricity prices, and the wage, then the pizza place owner ends up with half of the dollar (nominal) profits that he is accustomed to. But when the owner goes to buy gasoline, that price has halved, too, as has the rent and every other good. So, if before the deflation a single pizza gave enough profit to purchase a gallon of gas, then after the deflation a single pizza still gives enough profit to purchase a gallon of gas.

Keynes changed the pizza place example by supposing that prices of output adjust first, but two things prevent resource prices, including the wage, from changing quickly.

- The output (pizza) price falls. Firms must cut the wage since their output is now worth less. But workers mistake nominal wage cuts for real wage cuts—they don't understand that with half the money wages they can still make all the same purchases as before, since all the output is half price. They think they would be worse off with the wage cut and quit their jobs, looking for new jobs at the old, higher, nominal wages. Since all businesses face the same deflation, no business is hiring at the old, higher nominal wage, so the workers continue to be unemployed, searching for jobs that do not exist.

- Workers might have labor contracts. So when the pizza place owner says wages must be cut in half in order to keep producing pizzas, workers display the labor contract. With the lower price of pizza, the pizza place owner must shut down or cut back on output, firing workers.

However,

- The first point is difficult to support because Keynes did not explain how workers who mistook nominal wage cuts for real wage cuts could search for jobs at a nonexistent higher paying wages *for over a decade* (the length of The Great Depression), refusing to take a nominal cut. When asked, many people say that any workers who quit, rather than take the cut, would have to accept reality in a few months. If they face reality within six months, there is no recession. But The Great Depression lasted for over a decade.

- In addition, the second point is difficult to support. If labor contracts are a large problem for firms, firms go out of business, dissolving the restrictive contracts, leaving unemployed workers little choice but to find lower paying jobs. As soon as workers find jobs, the unemployment has ended and the economy is returned to potential.

Economics is a discipline that studies how self-interested individuals make decisions, doing their best to correctly respond to the incentives they face. But for long-term unemployment to be a problem, Keynes' individuals would rather stay unemployed with zero income than take a job earning less than they previously did—not responding to incentives and not learning from their experiences. So it is difficult to see how Keynes' model fits into economics.

Keynes said that the macroeconomy could fall into a bad short run equilibrium that lasted a long time and had high unemployment—a recession that employers and employees could not cure. Keynes called the difference between potential GDP and this recessionary equilibrium's GDP, "a **recessionary gap**." So if potential GDP is $18 trillion and our actual GDP is $16 trillion, in Keynes' language, we have a $2 trillion recessionary gap. In this recessionary gap, unemployment would be higher than the natural rate of 5.5%.

Keynes also said that an economy could get stuck with output above its potential, due to labor shortages, though he said these shortages would not last long, because wages would rise and eliminate the labor shortage. Keynes called the difference between potential GDP and the actual GDP in this situation an "**inflationary gap**." If potential GDP is $18 trillion and our actual GDP is $19 trillion, then we have a $1 trillion inflationary gap. In this inflationary gap, unemployment would be lower than the natural rate, of 5.5%.

KEYNES' REMEDY AND ITS PROBLEMS

Keynes said that The Great Depression was an example of labor markets that refused to adjust and that the most important way to remedy the economy was for government to spend, in order to hire the unemployed workers. Keynes also said one could use tax cut policies to help—leaving people more of their own income to spend on output, causing more hiring—but, Keynes worried that people might save their tax cuts, so he favored direct government spending. Note that Bastiat's idea that savings is spending, by another means, shows that savings is not a problem for the economy.

Keynes called the policy of using spending and taxes to cure inflationary and recessionary gaps "**fiscal policy**." He said that when the economy slumped into a recessionary gap, the government should spend more than it taxes, running a deficit, putting money into the economy to create employment and end the recession. In an inflationary gap, the government should tax more than it spends, running a surplus, taking money out of the economy to end the inflation.

Problem 1: Where does the money come from?

James Buchanan, the founder of the modern-day public choice school, which was discussed in Chapter 2, showed that Keynes' remedy of deficit spending during recessionary gaps *would* be followed, but his policy of running surpluses during inflationary gaps *would not* be followed. So Keynes gave politicians an excuse to run deficits, but his theory would not work as planned. Economists who realize that politicians avoid running surpluses must ask where the money to run deficits to cure recessionary gaps will come from. The possibilities follow:

- If government acquires the funds through taxes, it merely redirects spending as Bastiat cautions throughout his essay. Overall, there is no increase in spending.

- If government acquires the funds by money creation, then the increase in the money supply merely increases prices in the long run, leaving output unchanged. Friedman and Schwartz's 1971 book, *A Monetary History of the United States*, is unchallenged in its claim that money creation fuels inflation without increasing long run growth.

- If government acquires the funds by borrowing, then their increased demand for loanable funds will raise interest rates, as shown below. Government's $300 billion increase in demand for loanable funds (the distance between D and D2) raises interest rates from 6% to 7.5% on the graph. At the higher interest rates, there will be less private borrowing by businesses to invest—the funds that Microsoft would have borrowed are being borrowed by government. In addition, at the high interest rates, consumers borrow fewer funds to build houses and purchase automobiles. So, though the demand increased by $300 billion, the new equilibrium amount of loanable funds is only $150 billion higher. Businesses and firms have been **crowded out** of the loanable funds market. Besides this, the bonds eventually have to be paid back, which takes us back to the first point.

Figure 11.5

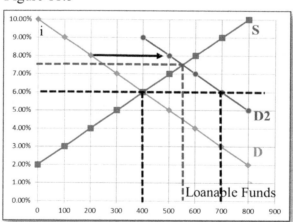

A final point to make about debt-financed spending is that it matters who finances the spending. If government spending is domestically financed, resources are withdrawn from the economy immediately, as per the discussion above. If government spending is financed by foreign borrowers, resources are withdrawn from the foreign economy immediately, so that crowding out only affects the domestic economy later, when the bonds are paid off. Either way, there is no free lunch. An economy must pay now or pay later.

The government of Greece, for example, borrowed heavily from foreign sources. They spent money on supporting 40% of the Greek population as government employees and to pay for Greece's social welfare system. Eventually the bonds had to be paid off and someone had to sacrifice to do so. The only country in Europe that could afford to make this sacrifice was Germany, but, in order to do so, Germans would have to sacrifice food, clothing, shelter, transportation, education, etc., to pay for decades of Greek overspending. Greece had to pay for most of their previous overspending, but Germans paid as well.

Problem 2: Keynes suffers from make-work fallacy

As Bastiat points out, individuals spend on goods they value, while government spends on goods that are politically expedient. However, Keynes did not think that the value of the goods and services that workers produced was of primary importance. He said,

> If the Treasury were to fill old bottles with banknotes, bury them at suitable depths in disused coalmines which are then filled up to the surface with town rubbish, and leave it to private enterprise on well-tried principles of *laissez-faire* to dig the notes up again… there need be no more unemployment and . . . the real income of the community, and its capital wealth also, would probably become a good deal greater than it actually is.
>
> *Keynes*

In saying this, Keynes perfectly fits Bastiat's stereotype of someone who labors under make-work fallacy—the idea that jobs have value other than the value of goods and services that the labor produces.

> The great Napoleon, it is said, thought he was doing philanthropic work when he had ditches dug and then filled in. He also said: "What difference does the result make? All we need is to see wealth spread among the laboring classes."
>
> *Bastiat*

Reading Exercise 11.1: Bastiat Chapter 5: Public Works http://www.econlib.org/library/Bastiat/basEss1.html [essential]

- What is Bastiat's test for which public works should be constructed?
- What is Bastiat's objection to people pointing out that government raises employment by constructing public works?
- What are the meanings of moonbeams and coins in Chapter 5?
- Bastiat says money creates an illusion. What ugly fact does Bastiat say the illusion hides?

Problem 3: Lags

The Economic Stimulus Act of 2008 was proposed in January, passed by both houses in one day and signed a week later. The bill authorized sending checks to taxpayers—calling the payments "tax rebates." The checks were from $300 to $1,200. People who did not even pay taxes could receive this "rebate." Payments began in early May and continued through August. Hence, from the idea being proposed to the plan being executed, nine months elapsed. This is a record short time for a fiscal policy action to be completed.

However;

- most recessions only last two quarters—six months, with only a few lasting nine months or more. So most recessions would be over by the time this record breaking fiscal policy action was completed.
- politicians, including those discussed, do not instantly know when an economic problem begins, so by the time they begin to discuss a remedy the problem may have cured itself

Fiscal policy is subject to the following lags:

- **The Data Lag**-the time it takes to realize there is a problem. If politicians only act when there is a recession, then they will act seven months after the recession starts—two quarters of decline have to be measured and it takes the data an extra month to come in. Most recessions have ended by this time.
- **The Legislative Lag**-politicians do not agree on spending and taxes and, even if they think there is a problem, will fight about it. Generally, any remedies will be in the next year's budget, which is scheduled to be passed by Congress by October 1st. If legislators realize there is a problem in April, perhaps their remedy can be applied six months later. However, if legislators begin their fight in November of one year and pass a remedy in the budget the next October, it will have taken a year.
- **The Transmission Lag**-Once the policy goes into effect, it takes time to execute. If politicians agree to spend $200 billion on highways, beginning January 1st, the workers will not be hired on January 2nd or even November 2nd.
  - Surveying must be done.
  - The property must be purchased
    - Government property lawyers must study every mile of the route, determining who owns which property
    - Appraisers must determine the value of the property
    - Lawyers must make offers to homeowners to voluntarily sell
    - Eminent domain actions must be completed for other homeowners
  - Environmental surveys must be completed on the route to determine that it does not harm endangered species or destroy wetlands. Lawsuits are often filed by those in the area, claiming that the road does harm to the environment, in order to discourage construction.
  - Bids must be taken for the construction—otherwise a politician may take a bribe to get the job for his crony friend. The bureaucracy must follow a complicated process involving considerations such as whether the construction company is unionized and whether the race of the company's owner is suitable to the state.
  - The construction company must build the road. Anyone who has seen a construction company work for two years repairing a twenty mile stretch of road knows that this step can take a while.
- **The Effectiveness Lag**-a completed project or policy does not instantly have its full effect. For instance, it may take investors a year or two to adjust to a new tax cut. It may take people a year or two to find out about a new consumer loan program.

A relatively quick fiscal policy project might have a 7 month data lag, plus a relatively quick 6 month legislative lag, plus a 12 month transmission lag, plus a 5 month effectiveness lag, totaling two and a half years of delay from when a problem starts to when fiscal policy has been fully applied. There is zero effect for over a year, with the effect building over the second year and completed by the two and a half year mark. By the time a new fiscal policy is taking good effect, the problem is over. Even with favorable lags like the short legislative and transmission lags listed above, the government is dumping spending into the economy at the wrong time, destabilizing the economy, rather than stabilizing it.

The 2009 stimulus package was intended to bring the US out of a recession that ended in June 2009, before hardly any of the $778 Billion had been spent. The Congressional Budget office estimated that 24% of the stimulus would be spent in all of 2009, 51% in 2010, and 25% over the next eight years. However, most of the 24% spent in 2009 involved handing money to states in order to pay unemployment benefits, enroll people for food stamps, and pay state Medicaid bills, not to build roads and bridges, putting people to work. In fact, given that a comfortable social safety net rewards not working, this spending may have been counterproductive.

The 2009 stimulus package was advertised as creating "shovel-ready" jobs. Lawmakers were literally told to pass it on Tuesday because they could not delay fixing the economy until Thursday when they had read the bill. The bill was passed into law before it was even fully compiled into one document by congressional secretarial services. That is, it was passed before it was truly written. However, the lags described above caused the "shovel" related jobs to be delayed for two to eight years. The President later said to his jobs council, "Shovel-ready was not as shovel-ready as we expected." http://www.youtube.com/watch?v=4p4-vPrcDBo [short reference video]

Those who understand Bastiat's critique cannot understand how fiscal policy could possibly be successful, since it merely redirects spending or creates inflation. Those who are not concerned about spending being redirected must, then, believe in make-work fallacy and dismiss government's calculation problem. And those who can ignore the first two issues must explain how the lags in the process are not relevant to fiscal policy. Someone who contends that Keynes' fiscal policy remedy is effective must deal with all three issues.

Paul Krugman, a well-known economist who writes an opinion column in the New York Times, displayed his love of broken windows as economic stimulus after the September 11th attacks by referring to the damage caused to New York. http://www.nytimes.com/2001/09/14/opinion/reckonings-after-the-horror.html [reference]

> First, the driving force behind the economic slowdown has been a plunge in business investment. Now, all of a sudden, we need some new office buildings. As I've already indicated, the destruction isn't big compared with the economy, but rebuilding will generate at least some increase in business spending.
>
> *Krugman*

THE GREAT DEPRESSION

Keynes wrote to explain the Great Depression. The above section on labor markets made clear that Keynes said that workers must refuse to work at lower paying jobs for years in order for his theory to explain the Great Depression. Robert Clower, a notable economist who wrote in the 20th century said, "There is no need to explain why the economy failed during the Great Depression because government failures explain it all." Here is the economic chain of events:

- Milton Friedman and Anna Schwartz showed in their *Monetary History of the United States* that the Great Depression began with large blunders by the Federal Reserve that destroyed much of the money supply and caused the banking crisis.

- The monetary and banking crises led to the stock market crash in 1929, greatly reducing US wealth.

- President Herbert Hoover created unprecedented government projects, raising government spending by 50%, to reduce unemployment—fiscal policy before Keynes.

- The crisis was made worse by passage of the Smoot-Hawley trade tariffs in 1930, which set off a world-wide trade war.

- Franklin Roosevelt changed the monetary system, confiscating the nation's gold, replacing it with a strictly paper money system that was, in name only, backed by gold.

- Franklin Roosevelt's New Deal shocked the economy with repeated tax changes, massive regulatory changes, far-reaching make-work projects, and lawsuits against companies. Jim Powell discusses some of the particulars. http://www.cato.org/publications/commentary/tough-questions-defenders-new-deal [essential]

Robert Higgs' research focuses on government changes that shocked the economy during The Great Depression, making it impossible for households and businesses to plan for the future. Higgs calls the confusion surrounding these shocks "**regime uncertainty**." He lists 40 pieces of legislation passed over an eight year period, which business could not foresee and could not easily adapt to, involving huge changes in existing taxes, new taxes, new regulations, and new government projects. As the war started and the New Deal ended, the following effects, cited by Higgs, took hold.

- World War II moved the administration's focus from the economy to enemy troops, entailing massive economic planning to fight the war. Historian Douglas Brinkley said, "By the end of 1943 . . . almost no real 'New Dealers' remained [in FDR's administration]." At the same time, consumers dealt with persistent shortages of food, fuel, and most other consumer goods caused by the war.

- After World War II, Keynes' followers predicted economic that disaster would occur when government spending fell. Paul Samuelson, a leading Keynesian said, "were we again planning to wind up our war effort in the greatest haste, to demobilize our armed forces, to liquidate price controls, to shift from astronomical deficits to even the large deficits of the thirties—then there would be ushered in the greatest period of unemployment and industrial dislocation which any economy has ever faced." The US government took the actions that Samuelson feared, but with none of the consequences he or other prominent Keynesians predicted. (http://econlog.econlib.org/archives/2010/07/paul_samuelsons.html) [reference]

- After WWII, congress cut business taxes from 90% to 38% and relaxed some of the regulations binding the economy. Kenneth Roose, writing in 1954, said, that the outlook was uncertain after the war, "but one of these uncertainties is not the type of economy in which business decisions are to be made." (cited in Higgs, below) People realized after Congress undid some of the New Deal that the US would not be a communistic country.

Though Robert Higgs coined the phrase "regime uncertainty," he did not invent the concept. http://www.independent.org/pdf/tir/tir_01_4_higgs.pdf [reference] Higgs cites a poll during the New Deal era that showed that businesspersons said FDR's administration was harming the economy by a margin of 65% to 26%. Another poll, taken at the beginning of the war, showed that 93% of businessmen expected less freedom after the war than before the war and 40% expected that government would dominate the economy, leaving, at most, a minor role for private business. Higgs quotes a top US investor, Lammot du Pont II, as saying about the New Deal,

> Uncertainty rules the tax situation, the labor situation, the monetary situation, and practically every legal condition under which industry must operate. Are taxes to go higher, lower or stay where they are? We don't know. Is labor to be union or nonunion? . . . Are we to have inflation or deflation, more government spending or less? . . . Are new restrictions to be placed on capital, new limits on profits? . . . It is impossible to even guess at the answers.
>
> *Lammot du Pont II*

SUPPLY SIDE ECONOMICS

Chapter 6 discussed monetary policy and this chapter has discussed Keynesian fiscal policy. Both are considered short run policies that have long run consequences. **Supply side economics** (SSE) is a long run policy in which the government reduces the cost of value creation through production and trade in order to promote more value creation. Government may lower the cost of value creation by reducing taxes and reducing regulation, increasing the ability and incentives to produce and trade.

In the labor market, the demand for labor increases, since business has more profitable opportunities and has more freedom to combine capital and labor in production. In addition, the supply of labor increases since lower payroll taxes and income taxes give households greater rewards from work. Both of these effects lead to an expansion of employment at stable wage rates.

If supply side policies work, then we should see gains in employment, new business creation, and business expansion that persist in the long run. These effects should not be accompanied by inflation either in the short run or the long run.

Figure 11.6

SSE concentrates on value creation, not on spending, as Keynesian economics does. In the view of supply side economists, spending is what happens as a result of value creation—spending does not cause value creation. Though the term was coined in the late 1970s to emphasize the difference between these policies and Keynesian, demand side, policies, the ideas regarding supply side economics draw from a long tradition of classical economics, which recognized that regulations and taxes suppressed economic growth. Daniel Webster, an early American legislator said, regarding the legality of taxation, "The power to tax is the power to destroy." Calvin Coolidge's Secretary of the Treasury, Andrew Mellon, recommended a large tax cut to spur economic growth, which it did, during the 1920's. And Bastiat likened taxes to evaporation which dries out otherwise fertile soil.

Whereas Keynesian economics depends on government's overcoming the calculation problem to plan the economy, SSE depends on the creativity of millions of people in the economy to plan.

Supply side economists cite Milton Friedman's **Permanent Income Hypothesis** in designing tax cuts. Friedman showed that a change in someone's after-tax income will affect their behavior if the increase is permanent, but not if the increase is temporary. Hence, SSE would not have recommended the 2008 stimulus "tax rebate" because it was a one-time change that would not seriously change individual behavior. It would not cause anyone to start a business, to expand their business, or to take a second job. Similarly, SSE would not have recommended the temporary cut in the Social Security tax (expired in January of 2012).

In addition, supply side economics only recommends changes in **marginal tax rates**—those that change as income, investment, or the other desired value creation activities change. If a consultant's total tax rate falls from 50% down to 28%, she may be willing to drive further, work harder, hire assistants, and advertise more in order to increase her consulting load. But if we simply lower her tax bill by $2,000, no matter how much she earns—a **lump sum tax cut**—this would not affect her willingness to expand her practice.

In addition, SSE advocates only **broad based tax cuts** which affect a wide range of economic activity, not **targeted tax cuts**—which only affect narrow categories activities that may or may not give incentives to create value. So advocates of SSE would not have recommended President Bush's tax credit for having a child because the credit would not, itself, cause someone to start a new business—it may cause them to be more likely to have children. In addition, SSE advocates would not have agreed with the $7,500 tax credit for purchasing an electric car that the 2009 stimulus package contained. This is not because SSE advocates dislike electric cars—they just recognize that any narrowly targeted tax cut is likely a victim of government's calculation problem. If electric cars have value and their production should be encouraged, then broadly based tax cuts will encourage their consumption and production, along with other goods and services.

The Laffer Curve

Opponents of SSE worry about tax cuts creating government budget deficits. But, as business expands and workers are hired, if the private market can create more value with the tax cut than the interest payments on the deficit, there is an overall gain to the economy, even if the deficit rises. However, Arthur Laffer pointed out that in some circumstances tax cuts do not even increase deficits.

The **Laffer Curve** shows the relationship between tax rates—the percentage paid—and tax revenues—the dollars the government receives. Suppose the tax rate is 0%. Clearly the government's tax revenues will be $0,

Figure 11.7

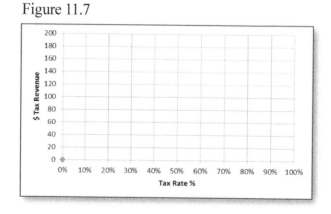

How much in taxes will the government collect if the tax rate is 100%? Many answer "all income." But

how much income will people earn if they know the tax rate is 100%? The answer is that if the tax rate is 100%, people will stop earning income. Perhaps they will do home production and work in the underground economy, but they will perform no work that will be taxed at 100%. So another point is on the following graph.

Figure 11.8

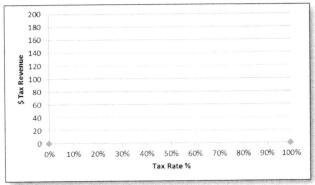

As the tax rate rises, we move to the right from 0%. This causes more money to come in to the government for a while, but eventually the tax rate gets so high that we discourage so much value creation and have so few people earning so little income, that tax revenue falls, eventually to zero.

Figure 11.9

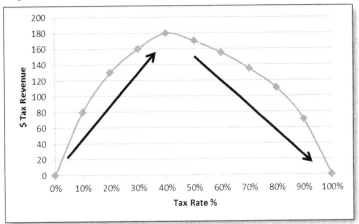

The curve need not be smooth nor symmetric. But we know that past some point, higher tax rates reduce economic activity so much that tax revenues fall. Hence, if we are to the right of the maximum of the Laffer curve, as we cut taxes, tax revenues rise.

When Ronald Reagan presented Laffer's ideas in 1980 his opponent, George Bush called them "Voodoo Economics." However, we see this effect in the tax cut that Andrew Mellon recommended in the 1920s, in Kennedy's 1960 tax cut, and in the two Reagan tax cuts of the 1980s, in Bill Clinton's capital gains tax cuts in the 1990s, and the Bush tax cuts of the 2000s.

Supply side economics relies on assumptions like, "people respond to incentives," "lower costs per unit encourage business to expand," "as business expands, more labor is hired," "people are willing to work more as the rewards to work increase," and "people work less as the rewards to work fall." These assumptions are harmonious with the longest traditions of economic thought.

The Federal Budget

DEFINITIONS AND RECENT HISTORY

The state spends and the state taxes. When the state spends more than it receives in taxes *in one year*, it runs a **deficit** equal to the amount of spending minus the amount of taxes. For a long time, government has run deficits, just as a person might charge more to their credit card than they pay off. The total amount that person owes on their credit card is their debt. The **federal debt** is the total amount the state owes. The way that the state spends more than it taxes is by selling government bonds to individuals, companies, and to other governments. So the federal debt is also the total amount of government bonds outstanding.

However, the federal debt is not the relevant amount that the US government owes, since the government owns some of its own bonds. Just as if a person owns his own IOUs, the portion of the US government's debt that the US government owns is irrelevant in any sense but an empty accounting sense. The **net public debt**—the portion of the debt that the US government owes *to others*, not to itself—is the relevant amount that the state owes. It is strange for a government to owe itself, but government does many strange things. This particular strange thing will be discussed later in the chapter.

In order to understand how big a burden debt is, we look at debt as a percentage of GDP. To relate this to a personal situation, paying off a $1 million dollar home is a small burden for a billionaire, but is a huge burden for a grocery clerk. Similarly, a small country like Portugal might have a crushing debt that the US could easily pay off, whereas the US debt would be unthinkable for a country like Portugal.

We will consistently use the language as outlined above, though that is not the way that government and the news media use the language—both are inconsistent. Much of the inconsistency comes from politicians wanting to change the language to obscure their actions.

- The government always has a spending plan, before they pass an actual budget. Suppose the government spent $3,700 billion in 2013 and plans to spend $3,950 billion in 2015. If a politician proposes that they change plans, and only spend $3,800 billion in 2015, they don't say, "We propose to spend $100 billion more than last year." They say, "We propose cutting spending by $150 billion," comparing the new spending to the spending plan, not to the previous spending.

- Government's plan is always a 10 year plan for spending, taxes, deficits and debt. When politicians really mean that they are going to cut their *planned* spending by $150 billion, as above, they typically say, "We will cut the debt by $1,500 billion," *citing the amount for the entire 10 years.* Also, they may, instead say, "We will cut the deficit by $1,500 billion," though the deficit is a yearly number.

- The first two points, taken together, can leave the public terribly uninformed. Perhaps the deficit is $1,300 billion and the public hears that their politician is going to cut the deficit by $1,500 billion. They logically conclude that the deficit will be eliminated. But, if the planned deficit is $1,550 billion, in reality, the yearly deficit will increase to $1,400 billion, since (1) the announced "cut" was a cut to a plan, not a cut compared to present, and (2) the announced "cut" is multiplied by 10 years, whereas the current deficit number is not.

- Finally, the chief forecaster of how new taxes and spending will affect the budget, the **Congressional Budget Office** (CBO), uses **static scoring**, which assumes that individuals will not change their behavior if taxation or spending changes. **Dynamic scoring**, on the other hand, looks at the effects of past changes on behavior to forecast the effects of new legislation. Here are two examples of static scoring.
  - If a 50% tax on investment income, which brings in $30 billion, is halved to 25%, the CBO estimates

that the tax revenue will fall to $15 billion, using static scoring. However, in reality, with lower taxes there will be more investment, so the 25% rate will apply to more dollars of investment than the old 50% rate. In fact, historically, when investment tax rates fall, investment tax revenue dollars often *rise* dramatically, as the Laffer Curve might predict. Similarly, if congress doubled the 50% tax rate to 100%, the CBO would estimate that tax revenues would double to $60 billion, though, in reality, investment would fall to $0, as would the tax revenue.

- If people currently spend $5 billion on eyeglasses every year, the CBO would expect that a new law that promises to buy eyeglasses for everyone would cost $5 billion. In reality, if the state buys eyeglasses for everyone, people will purchase more eyeglasses and sellers will raise prices, resulting in more than $5 billion in new spending. Dynamic scoring would try to take account of the behavior change in estimating the effects.

Here is our recent history, using the traditional language of yearly deficits, not 10 year debts and changes from the present levels of spending, not changes to future plans. Current data are compared to the year before the financial crisis to illustrate what has happened since then. The data are from the Economic Report of the President, Table B-19. (http://www.gpo.gov/fdsys/browse/collection.action?collectionCode=ERP) [reference for all data] These are measured in billions, so our spending in 2007 was a little above $2.5 trillion.

Table 12.1

	2007	2014 (est)
Taxes	$2,568	$3,002
Spending	$2,729	$3,651
Deficit	$161	$649
Net Public Debt	$5,035	$12,902
GDP	$14,028	$17,332
Debt as a % of GDP	35.9%	74.4%

This shows how dramatically the deficit and debt have risen since the financial crisis. It also shows the source of the rise—taxes **rose** by $430 billion per year, while spending rose by about $920 billion (nearly $1 trillion) per year.

The US currently spends about $10 billion per day. If the government confiscated the entire income of the 100 richest people, it would fuel spending for 24 days. Recent steps to cut spending or increase taxes have not been serious. Below are proposals for taxes and spending, along with how much time it would take the government to spend the proposed amount. (The sequester, a cut mentioned in the table, was passed, but has now been partially repealed.)

Table 12.2

Tax or Spending Proposal	Status	Govt Would Spend the $ in
Minimum tax rate for wealthy (Buffett Rule)	Campaign talking point	2 days
Eliminate oil and gas tax breaks	Campaign talking point	32 seconds
Eliminate private jet tax breaks	Campaign talking point	26 seconds
Let "Bush tax cuts for the wealthy" expire	End of 2012, deal done	8 days
"The sequester" spending cut (but scaled back)	Ongoing spending deal	8 days
2010 Republican promise to cut spending	Campaign talking point	10 days
2011 compromise on the 2010 promise	Negotiated settlement	3 days
Actual cuts from the 2010 promise	Actual cut	43 seconds

HISTORICAL SPENDING, DEBT, AND DEFICITS

Historical Debt

The graph below reveals that WWII gave the US a huge increase in the net public debt. After WWII GDP increased quicker than the Net Public Debt, so the ratio fell. During the 1980s the percentage began to decline, then, after the Soviet Union fell, military spending fell. At the same time, congress slowed the growth of spending. Since GDP increased strongly during this time, the percentage shrank. The size of the debt, compared to the economy was stable during the early 2000s, but then increased during the crisis of 2008 due to (1) falling GDP and (2) the $152 billion stimulus of 2008 (mentioned in the previous chapter). Currently the net public debt, as a percentage of GDP, is about the same as in 1950.

Figure 12.1

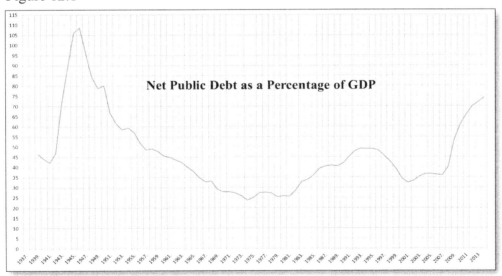

In the years since 2008 the ratio increased quickly as spending rose by large amounts due to:

- The $778 billion stimulus package of 2009,
- Building part of the stimulus into the "baseline" so that it became regular yearly spending and refusing to pass another budget for years, to avoid debating the issue,
- Two 8% increases in ordinary spending in 2009,
- TARP funds that were spent and not repaid, and

- Various increases in spending, such as increasing unemployment insurance from a 26 week program to a 99 week program and the new health care law.

Historical and Future Spending

Historically, US government spending was about 1-2% of GDP. This increased greatly during the Civil War and WWI, but fell after the wars. The debt explanation above applies to the graph as well.

Figure 12.2

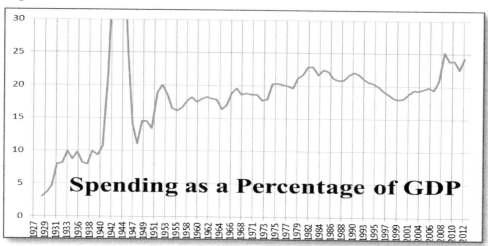

Historically, we mostly spent on military goods. However, the New Deal normalized the concept of socialized costs—spreading private costs to society, in general, through taxation—with Social Security being the large social program from the era. Unemployment insurance and a host of other accompanying socializations of private costs accompanied social security. Kennedy proposed Medicare and Medicaid in the early 1960's and Lyndon Johnson pushed them through congress.

Currently we spend

- 60% on transfers such as Social Security, Medicare, Medicaid, Unemployment Insurance and other welfare programs,
- 20% on national defense,
- 5% on interest on the debt, and
- 15% on everything else, such as roads, education, prisons, judicial system, department of energy, agriculture, environmental protection, NASA, etc.

Our spending patterns are shown below. This is a stacked graph in which the height of each colored area shows the percentage of the budget that each component takes up—so they all add up to 100% of the budget at all times.

Figure 12.3

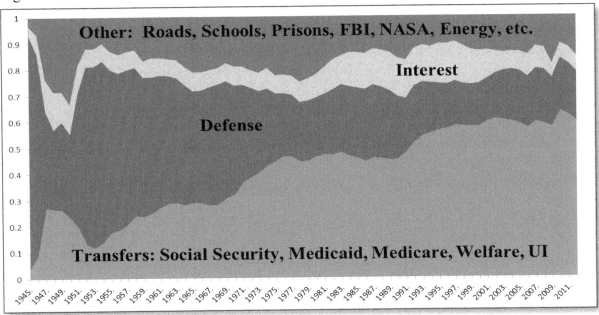

The interest component of spending is low at the moment because the Fed has expanded the money supply so greatly in recent times, lowering rates to 1% and less. However, when inflation threatens and the Fed lowers the money supply, raising rates toward 4%, a historically moderate rate, this part of spending will rise drastically, causing a crisis. However, this is not the major crisis that awaits US government spending.

The first page of the chapter mentions that the US government owns some of its own debt—as if you had a shoebox of IOU's written by you, to you, under the bed. These IOUs would not actually represent wealth that you own or debts that you owe. You cannot pay the rent with them. This box of IOUs is analogous to the US government's "trust funds," including the Social Security, Medicare, and Medicaid trust funds. Here is the "theory" behind them.

If $807 billion in SS taxes is collected and $686 billion in benefits are paid, $121 billion remain after payments are made. The government, in theory, saves the $121 billion by printing up government bonds and setting them aside. In reality, government prints the bonds and spends the $121 billion. We know that SS taxes will eventually fall behind benefits paid, so at that time the government will "cash the bonds in" to pay the benefits. But, to whom will the government "cash the bonds in?" To themselves—as if you were cashing in your own IOUs, to yourself, to pay the rent. Hence, *for purposes of paying benefits, there are $0 actual dollars in the trust fund*, even though the Social Security Administration owns $2.7 trillion worth of bonds.

Social Security was never actuarially sound—it could not do what it promised to do over the long run. However, FDR and his "New Deal" secretary of labor ignored the long term consequences. The inevitable end of the program was put off for decades by (1) the baby boom after WWII and (2) the massive entry of women into the workforce. But the baby boom was destined to turn into the geriatric boom, turning salvation into doom, and there were only so many women to enter the workforce.

Today, Social Security retirement benefits average $1,200 per retiree. If there were 50 workers per retiree, as existed in 1950, this would amount to $24.00 per worker. But today there are 3 workers per retiree, averaging $400/worker. In fifteen years there will be 2 workers per retiree, averaging $600 per worker—a 50% increase in payments.

Medicare and Medicaid have even worse problems, since the socialization of medicine has caused costs to rise. Government fights the problems caused by socialism with more socialism, though—not by eliminating the socialist aspects of policy—so costs still rise and are passed on to those who did not incur them. While the public believes that many cannot afford medicine without socialization of medicine, they do not see that the reason that costs are so high is that people who spend other people's money do not care about costs, nor do those whom they do business with.

Here is a quote from the Social Security and Medicare Trustees report—which is signed by three of the president's cabinet and three actuaries.

> Both Medicare and Social Security cannot sustain projected long-run program costs under currently scheduled financing, and legislative modifications are necessary to avoid disruptive consequences for beneficiaries and taxpayers.
>
> Lawmakers should not delay addressing the long-run financial challenges facing Social Security and Medicare. If they take action sooner rather than later, more options and more time will be available to phase in changes so that the public has adequate time to prepare. Earlier action will also help elected officials minimize adverse impacts on vulnerable populations, including lower-income workers and people already dependent on program benefits.   *Social Security and Medicare Trustees Report*

(http://www.ssa.gov/oact/trsum/) [reference]

Things are even worse than this because the actuaries must make all the assumptions of governmental accounting such as (1) benefits can be paid out of trust funds made up of government bonds (not of money) and (2) politicians make cuts to future benefits early in every year, which would result in less future spending—even though those lawmakers restore the benefit cuts at the end of every year, before the future cuts can be made. The trend in the debt graph above is expected to worsen—with the three programs growing even faster. The long term debt of the three programs is estimated to be $220 trillion—many times greater than GDP. (http://www.cato.org/blog/washington-big-spenders-wasteful-essential) [reference]

<u>Historical Taxes</u>

Except in times of war, the US historically had balanced budgets, so spending was equal to taxes at about 1-2% of GDP, with revenues coming mainly from import tariffs. The income tax amendment was passed in 1913 and expanded to nearly 80% of income during WWI, but only the very wealthy paid income taxes at first. Under the leadership of Andrew Mellon, Treasury Secretary to Harding and Coolidge, taxes fell continuously through the 1920s, eventually down to 24%.

Figure 12.4

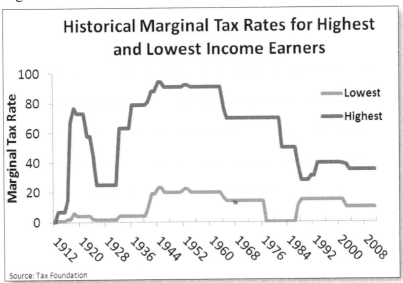

During the New Deal , tax rates tripled, then increased up to 90% during WWII and stayed there until Kennedy cut them to 70% in the mid-60s (Kennedy proposed, Johnson pushed through congress). Under Reagan, the top rate fell to 50% in 1982, then to 28% in 1988. Clinton raised rates to 40%, Bush lowered them to 35%, then Obama raised them back to 40%.

Given the way tax rates changed, someone using static scoring—which assumes that people's behavior does not change when their incentives change—one would expect that tax revenues, as a percentage of GDP would look the same. However, people respond to incentives, so that the substantive tax cuts of Kennedy, Reagan, and Bush did not lower revenues as a percentage of GDP, as seen below.

Figure 12.5

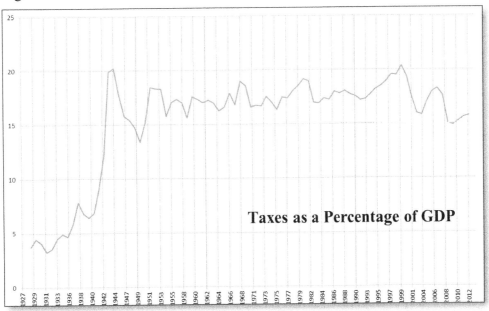

We see tax revenues fall before Kennedy's tax cuts, but rise afterward. In general, we see taxes rise and fall with economic problems, such as those in the early 70s and in the late 70s, but as the economy recovers tax revenues rise. Similarly, tax revenues fell with the recession before Reagan's cuts, but rose afterward, and continued to rise in the 1990s. Tax revenues fell with the "dot-com" meltdown of the late 1990s and in the subsequent recession, but rose after the Bush tax cuts of 2003. People may quibble about exact timing, but the fact remains that the two graphs above do not look alike, as static scoring would imply. People behave dynamically, responding to incentives, starting businesses and hiring employees if they think they can profit, after taxes. So tax revenues are not the same as tax rates—a point lost on politicians and the public.

Tax revenues rose during WWII and stabilized at about 17-18% of GDP, even though taxes were collected at all the tax rates listed above—from 28% up to 90%. The fact that, no matter how high *rates* go, tax *revenues* stay in the 17-18% range, is called Hauser's Law. Hauser's Law implies that we cannot balance our spending problems with tax increases, above a certain point. The spending graph, above, shows that the US government is currently spending 25% of GDP, far above its taxes of 16% of GDP. Hauser's law says that if we are to close that gap, it must be with spending cuts, not tax increases.

Tax Fairness

The chapter on socialism and capitalism contains a brief discussion of fairness. Briefly, people differ on whether fairness means that the rules/laws are the same for everyone or whether the outcomes are the same for everyone—whether everyone has the same income, for instance. A professor who is concerned with equality of outcomes might give everyone the class average. A professor who is concerned with equal opportunities might be careful that each section of her course has the same amount of time to take the test.

Those who favor equalized outcomes with regard to economic wellbeing favor the state's redistributing income from those with high incomes and to those with low incomes. As in the socialism chapter, when value creation is divorced from rewards, less value creation through trade and production takes place, meaning lower consumption, in general, and fewer jobs.

- A **proportional tax** is one in which the tax rate is the same at all income levels.
- A **progressive tax** is one in which the tax rate rises as income rises.
- A **regressive tax** is one in which the tax rate rises as income falls.

There are two important words that are sometimes overlooked in the above definitions—"rate" and "income." Carefully consider both words in working the following exercise.

Thinking Exercise 12.1 Progressivity

- Suppose that a particular tax takes $5,000 from a taxpayer with an income of $50,000 and takes $10,000 from a taxpayer with an income of $150,000. Is this tax proportional, progressive, or regressive?

- Consider the percentage of one's income paid to the cigarette tax. Is the cigarette tax proportional, progressive, or regressive?

- Reconsider your answer. Suppose that both you and Bill Gates smoked 1 pack per day. Who would pay the biggest proportion of their income to the government based on the cigarette tax?

- Are sales taxes proportional, progressive, or regressive?

- Who saves a bigger percentage of income, rather than consuming it and subjecting it to the sales tax—those with high incomes or those with low incomes? Are sales taxes proportional, progressive, or regressive?

- The Social Security Tax and other taxes are on wage income only. Are they proportional, progressive, or regressive? Consider how much of a person's income is wage income—comparing wealthy taxpayers to others.

- Is the income tax proportional, progressive, or regressive? Why might someone think the income tax is regressive—that those with high incomes pay low percentages of their income to the government in income taxes?

Many claim that the US income tax structure is regressive because wealthy people hire expensive lawyers and accountants to shield their incomes from taxes. The issue is whether they can legally shield enough to compensate for the higher legal rates on high incomes. The question can only be answered by data. If the income tax were proportional, then those earning 20% of the income would pay 20% of the taxes. Here is the IRS data.

Table 12.3

Income Group	Group's Share of Income	Group's Share of Fed. Income Taxes	Income One Must Earn to be in Group
Top 1%	20%	38%	$380,000
Top 10%	46%	70%	$113,800
Top 25%	70%	86%	$67,280
Top 50%	87%	98%	$33,000
Bottom 50%	13%	2%	Less than $33,000

Since high income people pay a higher share of taxes than they have of income, the income tax is progressive—in fact, it is highly progressive. The bottom 50% of income earners pay almost no income taxes.

Many claim that, though income taxes may be progressive, when one includes payroll taxes, such as Social Security, Unemployment Insurance, Medicare, and the like, that the total federal tax system is regressive. The following table comes from the latest study on the subject by the Congressional Budget Office.

Figure 12.6

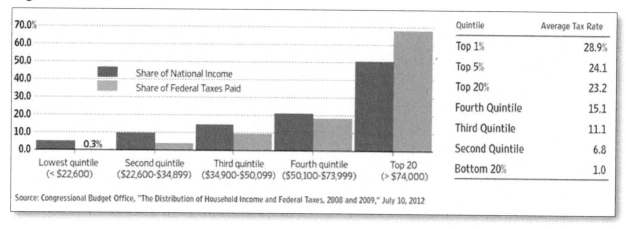

Source: Congressional Budget Office, "The Distribution of Household Income and Federal Taxes, 2008 and 2009," July 10, 2012

We can see here, as well, that at low levels of income the share of income exceeds the share of total federal taxes, while at high levels the share of taxes exceeds the share of income. In the table to the right of the chart shows that the top 1% pays a tax rate of 28.9%, while the bottom 20% pays an average tax rate of 1%. Hence, it is *not true* that all federal taxes, taken together, are regressive.

It is the case that some individual taxpayers who have high incomes can structure their earnings so that they pay little in taxes. But it is not true, in general.

Friedman on Taxes, Spending, and Deficits

If a government leader wished to improve the economy, should she advocate reforms in (1) spending (2) taxes or (3) deficits. The three are related, but they are not the same thing.

The chapter on macroeconomic adjustment made the points that deficits have costs:

- With domestically financed government spending, resources are withdrawn from the economy immediately.
- With foreign financed government spending, resources are withdrawn immediately from the foreign economy, so that crowding out affects the domestic economy *later*, when the bonds are paid off.
- With government spending financed by money creation, in the long run there is no effect other than to create inflation and destabilize the economy as prices cease to reflect value. Friedman's "helicopter drop" is the most clear short run analysis—in the short run there may be some simulative effect from money creation, but in the long run money creation only causes inflation.

Spending could also be financed by taxes, but, as the chapter on public choice made clear, taxes have costs, since they make it more expensive to create value, which also results in lower employment.

If our leader can only pick one issue—spending, taxes, or deficits, Milton Friedman's advice is of use. He said that because it is so inefficient for one person to spend another's income on a third person, such spending destroys value. Friedman concluded that this destruction is so great that it is better to lower spending than to lower deficits. So if our new leader faces a choice between the following two economic plans, that we should prefer Plan 2.

Table 12.4

	Spending	Taxes	Deficit
Plan 1	$900 billion	$900 billion	$0
Plan 2	$500 billion	$300 billion	$200 billion

With Plan 2, less of the economy suffers from the three-party spending problem, hence more value will be created. Since, in the long run, the $200 billion must be paid off, it would be better increase productivity now to help to pay off the long run deficit.

IN SUMMARY

This text has been devoted to lessons on how individuals interact in markets to improve their lives. The text's outlook favors free markets, focused on logical argument and examples of how people who interact freely with each other can make their lives better. However, given that markets are not fully free, the text also discusses the effects of the state on individuals and on their economic interactions. The aim of the text has been to help you to understand the economic world around you as you find your place in the spontaneous order of the market.

All the best.

CPSIA information can be obtained
at www.ICGtesting.com
Printed in the USA
FSOW04n0102230417
33303FS